When Living Hurts

A Publication of the YAD TIKVAH FOUNDATION

Acknowledgments

This book is in a true sense a collective work and is dedicated to the members of the UAHC Task Force on Teen Suicide—a project of the Yad Tikvah Foundation—and the many young people who wrote to us with their suggestions to enhance the quality of this new edition.

This edition is based largely on the original text by Dr. Sol Gordon.

Sol Gordon

When Living Hurts

A lively *what-to-do book* for yourself
or someone you care about who feels
 discouraged ✦ *sad* ✦ *lonely* ✦ *hopeless* ✦
 angry or frustrated ✦ *unhappy or*
 bored ✦ *depressed* ✦ *suicidal*

FOR TEENAGERS
AND YOUNG ADULTS

Revised Edition

UAHC Press ✦ New York, New York

Library of Congress Cataloging-in-Publication Data

Gordon, Sol, 1923–
  When living hurts: a lively what-to-do book for yourself or
someone you care about who feels discouraged, sad, lonely, hopeless,
angry or frustrated, unhappy or bored, depressed, suicidal / Sol
Gordon.—Rev. ed.
       p. cm.
    "For teenagers and young adults."
    Includes bibliographical references.
    ISBN (invalid) 0-8074-0501-1 (acid-free paper): $10.00
    1. Youth—Suicidal behavior.   2. Suicide—Prevention.
3. Adolescent psychology.   I. Title.
HV6546.G67   1994
616.85′844505′0835—dc20   94-14153
                                                            CIP

This book is printed on acid-free paper

Feldman Library

I write for young people of all faiths,
little faith, no faith, and for those still searching.
I wrote to encourage you to stand for *something*;
otherwise you may fall for anything.

—Sol Gordon

Believe that life is worth living and your belief
will help to create the fact.

—William James

The secret of wisdom is kindness.

—Charles B. Haywood

Advice from a teenager
who has attempted suicide:
No matter how bad things may seem,
they will get better. Just hold on.

Nobody is weirder than anyone else—some people
just take longer to understand.

—Tom Robbins
Even Cowgirls Get the Blues

The great Jewish sage Hillel used to say:
If I am not for myself, who will be for me?
And if I am only for myself, what am I?
And if not now, when?

What do I think Hillel says to us now?
There is an ever-present need to enhance ourselves
and our spiritual aspirations, but we must never forget
our obligations to society lest we discover one day that
it is too late.

What does Hillel say to you?

Contents

When Living Hurts

Introduction

This is a book for people who want to help others who are in trouble.

It is also for people who are lonely, depressed, or suicidal.

My basic message is that we are all our brothers' and sisters' keepers and that living well is the best antidote for hopelessness, helplessness, feeling unloved, unfairness, and tragedy. This book focuses on how to cope with disappointments and imperfections (in an imperfect world).

Most other how-to books tell you

- not to worry. (When's the last time someone told you not to worry and you stopped?)
- not to feel guilty. (If you've done something wrong, maybe you should feel guilty.)
- that you can be anything you want to be. (You should live so long.)
- to get rid of unrealistic expectations. (How does one know in advance that one's expectations are unrealistic?)
- that if you eliminate shoulds, musts, perfectionistic tendencies, worries, and other imperfections, you'll be happy. (So what else is new?)

The plain fact is that life, in large part, is made up of

things to worry about—not only personal things but the state of the world, including hunger, overpopulation, torture, crime-infested cities, disasters, personal tragedies, and despair.

Life can be unfair, unlucky, uninteresting, and unnerving for large parts of the day or for years.

Real people have bad moods, experience periods of depression, and fall in love with people who don't love them.

Life can also be full of joys, pleasures, and excitement. These sensations may not last long, but they, nevertheless, are real.

Most other self-help books want you to pretend that you can change reality by changing how you feel about it. This book does not pretend. It acknowledges the pain of the real world, but it also says that by being helpful to others, by reaching out beyond your own pain, you can renew and revitalize yourself.

Fragments of
an Autobiography

Sometimes one finds oneself in a grim situation. There is nothing one can do about it except to wait for a brighter future. I remember my own childhood as a sad and lonely time. I hated school and often was in conflict with my parents. I contemplated suicide and imagined that everybody would be sorry. It was hard not thinking about irrational ways out of my situation.

I began to feel better in my late teen years when I realized that there is nothing wrong with being unhappy every once in a while. God knows, there are lots of times when being unhappy is the most appropriate response.

I figured out that it was not difficult to tell when unhappiness is based on irrationality. Irrational unhappiness comes equipped with symptoms like depression, fear of high or closed places, pains without actual disease, feelings of anxiety, despair, and emptiness, an inability to feel motivated, a gross loss of appetite, or sexual compulsions. Unhappy people have a tendency to be mean and abusive to their close ones.

Rational unhappiness is mostly grand, dignified, private, a bit heroic, unselfish, free of irrational guilt or pride. It ends up being a learning experience . . . however much a person may have suffered. For example: You break up with your boyfriend or girlfriend. You are in pain, but you make every effort not to cause others pain as well. You use this time to reexamine your goals in life.

What to Do If You or a Friend Needs Help

Do you have a good reason to feel bad?

Lesley Hazleton writes:

> To be fully alive means to experience the full range of emotions, to struggle with the downs as well as to enjoy the ups. Life is certainly difficult and even unpredictable—full of meaning and purpose at one time and utterly meaningless and purposeless at another, sometimes so desirable that we wish to freeze it at a certain point and remain there forever, and at other times so undesirable that we may find ourselves wishing we had never been born. But it also has its own dynamics. There is no real happiness without the experience of depression to balance it. If we are not capable of depression, we are not capable of happiness either. In a very real sense, depression keeps us alive.
>
> *The Right to Feel Bad—Coming to Terms with Normal Depression,* Dial Press, 1984

Almost everyone feels bad, down, or miserable occasionally. Ordinary depression strikes everyone from time to time. But some of us suffer from it more often than others.

This book is not concerned with temporary upsets, such as an event that was spoiled by the weather or someone's bad mood. Such feelings are responses to real situations and usually don't last long or cause symptoms like fears and physical problems.

The depression this book is concerned with results from irrational ideas, such as blaming yourself for something that you were not responsible for—all those "should've," "could've," or "would've" situations in your life. Depression generally occurs because, for one reason or another, you feel inferior. Perhaps you relentlessly compare yourself unfavorably to others.

There will always be people who are luckier, richer, better looking, or smarter than you are. Even so, each person is unique. No one in the world is exactly like you. Could it be that we are all on earth for a special mission or purpose? As Eleanor Roosevelt once said, "No one can make you feel inferior without your consent." Of course, this is easier said than accepted.

It's important to deal with depression as early as possible because it can lead to serious problems, such as headaches, backaches, fears, obsessions, nightmares, insomnia, or a chronic state of feeling hopeless and inferior. There is hardly anything more exhausting than feeling inferior.

Many people deal with feelings of depression in the wrong way. They eat too much or too little. Or they think alcohol or drugs can numb their feelings. Alcohol and drugs might make you feel good for a little while, but then you usually feel worse than before. You have a hangover and you feel bloated, terrible, alone, and miserable.

What should you do if you're feeling depressed?

THERE IS HARDLY ANYTHING
MORE ENERGIZING
THAN LEARNING SOMETHING NEW.
IT'S THE FIRST STEP IN
GETTING OUT OF A DEPRESSION.

Here are some suggestions to get you started.

- Write a letter to someone who would be surprised to hear from you.
- Go to a park, a museum, a play, or somewhere you rarely think of going.
- Watch a program on TV that you wouldn't ordinarily watch, like a PBS documentary or "Northern Exposure."
- Go see a serious movie.
- Don't watch TV for a whole day. (Better yet, don't watch for a whole week.) Find out what radio has to offer aside from your favorite music.
- Bake bread or cookies from scratch.
- Write down all the things that you like to do. Don't stop until you've written down at least a number equivalent to your age. If you are twenty years old, you should be able to write down twenty things you really enjoy. Then without giving the matter much thought, *do* one of the things on your list.
- Daydream without feeling guilty.
- Fix or build something.
- Write a haiku (a seventeen-syllable poem having three lines containing usually five, seven, and five syllables respectively).
- Purchase a magazine that you haven't read before, like

Ms., *Rolling Stone,* or *Psychology Today,* and read at least two articles in it.
- Create your own psychodrama. Act out a role for at least twenty minutes that you would like to play in real life. Strive to be very animated and enthusiastic.
- Get a dog or cat or some tropical fish.
- Make a decision to collect something (stamps, coins, cactus plants).
- If nothing else works, try exercise.

This list is a start. In the long run there is no substitute for feeling good about yourself. This happens mainly when you have a sense of purpose or a mission in your life—a feeling that life is worthwhile because your life is meaningful!

Caution: Don't fall for the trap of equating self-esteem with "feeling good about yourself," which can sometimes result in selfish, greedy, and uncaring behavior. It is surprising how many people feel good about themselves while putting down those around them.

When you feel "top-notch" about yourself, you have energy, you are optimistic, and you treat the people around you with kindness. I like the definition of *self-esteem* that was developed by the California Legislative Task Force on Self-Esteem (1990): "Appreciating my own worth and importance and having the character to be accountable for myself and to act responsibly toward others."

IF YOU HAVE AN INTEREST,
PEOPLE WILL BE INTERESTED IN YOU.
IF YOU ARE DEPRESSED,
YOU WILL BE DEPRESSING TO BE WITH.

You'll start feeling better when you put a little effort into learning something new; when you feel good about doing something for someone else; when you begin to plan ahead instead of worrying ahead; and most of all when you stop comparing yourself to other people.

If you've been depressed for a long time and are not sure why, schedule a complete medical examination. Something may be physically wrong with you that is affecting your mental state.* Medication might help but only temporarily. Get into therapy or seek counseling with a person you trust. You may find that you are able to confide more in a professional than in someone you know. Professionals are trained to listen and be helpful. We can't always say that about friends. A warning: Don't stay with a therapist that you don't like. Think twice about continu-

*For more information about depressive illness, call 1-800-248-4344.

ing to see someone if you haven't experienced a significant improvement after about ten sessions. For most people some improvement is evident early in the treatment. In addition, read carefully the sections of this book that are pertinent to you.

If you have a friend who is depressed, you are probably concerned about how that person is managing when you are not around. You may want to keep tabs on your friend without making it seem that you are invading his or her privacy. Try to be supportive and available to talk about your friend's situation and feelings, and when you leave his or her company, be sure you say something that lets your friend know you are still with him or her in spirit. To convey your availability, say something like:

- "Call me if you want to talk or get together."
- "I can't know how you actually feel, but I do know it's tough for you right now. I hope you will share your feelings with me."
- "I'm your friend. I care for you."

Whatever words you use, be sure your friend knows that you care and are ready to help.

Are you lonely?

The most painful kind of loneliness is the loneliness that makes you feel hopeless and desperate as a result of low self-esteem.

Strangely enough, the loneliest people often feel the most unhappy when they are among others, even in crowds. Some of the loneliest people I know are married and have families.

Loneliness is a state of mind. Well-adjusted people often enjoy being alone. They even savor the precious moments when they are alone, using the time to read, reflect, or just relax. It is their choice.

It's a different matter if you are alone without wanting to be. But even when you are alone, it is important to remember that loneliness is a state of mind. You can put being alone to good use. There are lots of things you can do when you are by yourself.

- Read.
- Keep a daily journal.
- Listen to your favorite music.
- Eat and dress well.
- Treat yourself to a leisurely bath.
- Clean your room (apartment).
- And you know what? It's okay to talk to yourself. (You can figure out a lot of things that way!)
- Call a cousin whose company you enjoy and plan on getting together.
- Look over the family photo album.
- Watch a Chaplin or Marx Brothers film on your VCR.

Although it's hard to think about reaching out to others when we feel lonely, changing our focus can really help. But it does take some motivation.

For some people loneliness lasts a long time. I was lonely most of my childhood. I wasn't good at athletics. Kids made fun of me because I was a redhead. I was clumsy. I survived by daydreaming and reading books. In my late teens I went to libraries and museums, where I talked to people. It was in a museum that I met one of my best friends. As my life improved at home and school, I started to see things differently. Exactly how it all happened I am not sure. I only know that life became good once more.

IF YOU SHOW INTEREST IN OTHERS, OTHERS WILL BE INTERESTED IN YOU.

Below is a list of books to read and tapes to study while you are passing from a "loneliness" stage into a "pleasurable aloneness" stage.

Those who are into reading might try
- *Whoever Said Life Was Fair* by Sara Kay Cohen
- *On Caring* by Milton Mayeroff
- *The Art of Worldly Wisdom* by Baltasar Gracien
- *When Bad Things Happen to Good People* by Harold S. Kushner
- *The Different Drum* by M. Scott Peck
- *The Measure of Our Success* by Marian Wright Edelman

Novels that deal with the purpose of life include
- *The Color Purple* by Alice Walker
- *The Snow Leopard* by Peter Matthiessen
- *The Book of Laughter and Forgetting* by Milan Kundera
- *Siddhartha* by Herman Hesse

I also recommended novels by Tim O'Brien, Russell Banks, E. L. Doctorow, Kurt Vonnegut, Herman Melville,

Saul Bellow, Virginia Woolf, Amos Oz, I. B. Singer, Ernest Hemingway, and Elie Wiesel.

Russell Baker's autobiography *Growing Up* is inspirational, as is Eudora Welty's *One Writer's Beginnings*. Paul Cowan's *An Orphan in History* probably would interest anyone concerned about his or her Jewish identity.

Don't feel like reading? Then get the magazine *Psychology Today*. It always lists self-help tapes. Order ones by Albert Ellis, David Burns, William Glasser, Rollo May, Jack Gibb, and Jean Houston. Look carefully at the titles and choose those that respond best to your present situation.

If you are not into reading, that's okay. You could move into fitness and exercise to build your body. Or you might try meditation or yoga. You could even find out more about your religion.

- Take emotional and intellectual risks. Unless you are willing to risk being rejected, you will never know the joy of feeling accepted.
- Try to do the right thing for yourself. You can't live trying to measure up to other people's expectations.
- If you feel attractive, you'll attract people. If you feel unattractive, you'll give off bad vibrations.
- Loneliness is a temporary state. Use the time to be nice to yourself. Don't be mean to your family. If you are lonely, it's not somebody else's fault.
- A person who fails at something is not a failure. Failure is an event, not a person.

No matter what your problem is, you can't solve it with alcohol, speed, coke, crack, or grass. Even if you are able to continue functioning, you'll become less productive, as well as nasty to people who care about you. You'll spoil any chances you might have had for a good sex life and an intimate relationship.

People who are hooked characteristically
- lie a lot
- can't be trusted (because they frequently make and break promises)
- are overconfident (and tend to say things like "Don't worry, I can handle it")
- give priority to the addiction (over everything else in their life, including intimate relationships)
- have poor judgment (which makes it dangerous for them to drive)

Eight key messages about
drug and alcohol abuse

- If you drink, don't drive.
- If someone says in a loud defensive voice, "I'm not drunk. I can drive!" he or she is drunk and shouldn't drive.
- If one or both of your parents are alcoholics, it is best to avoid drinking altogether.
- Alcohol, illegal drugs, and legal ones, such as cigarettes, are all poison to the unborn. They can lead to a variety of birth defects that drastically affect the entire life of a baby.
- One small mistake, like driving while drunk, can take or seriously impair your life and the lives of innocent people.
- One or two drinks can, as Shakespeare wrote, "provoke the desire" but more than that will "take away the performance." Impotence (the inability to maintain an erection) often occurs if a man drinks too much and then tries to have sex.
- People in the chronic stages of alcoholism begin to act like their own worst enemy (behavior that is called "identification with the aggressor" by psychologists) and seriously damage their health, resulting in their premature death.
- People "under the influence" are high risks for exposure to unprotected sex and HIV/AIDS.

Please note: Until addicts start to deteriorate from the effects of drugs, they often appear to be nice, lively, interesting people. That's why it's easy for them to fool almost everybody. They usually don't need understanding. What they need is help.

If you can't stop drinking or using drugs on your own (or if your friend can't), a Crisis Intervention Clinic will tell you where you can get help. Once you are addicted or a chronic user of any drug, it's difficult to stop without professional support. Getting help is an act of courage. Not getting help leads to despair and hurting the people you care about the most.

Here is something else you need to know. Just getting off the stuff will not automatically solve your problems. You will still need time, patience, energy, and motivation to make new friends and develop new interests. The most difficult period is the first three or four weeks after stopping. This is a period of high anxiety and tension. It's the time you should learn something new, discover a hobby, try a new sport, exercise a lot, or get involved helping others who are worse off than you are. Above all, don't expect to be perfect and don't expect anyone to appreciate what you are trying to accomplish. It is a gift that you are giving yourself.

Learning to cope with this transitional period of anxiety is just as important as stopping substance abuse. Otherwise you might start again. But even if you do start again (and many do), you need to keep in mind that you can always stop again.

The main thing is to get help *right away*. A group such as Alcoholics Anonymous is a good place to start. If you are not into a religious-oriented approach, try an alternative recovery group. Start by reading *The Small Book* by Jack Trimpey (Delacorte, 1992).

Maybe you *are* too fat or too skinny or too tall or too short. Or maybe you think that some part of you is not just "right," for example, your thighs, nose, arms, or hair. Maybe it's all in your imagination or maybe it's due to lack of information. Perhaps you can't change certain aspects of your appearance, but you can change your attitude about how you look.

The first thing you need to know is that people who accept themselves are attractive to other people. It's not true that short, fat, or "unattractive" people can't "find" a mate or a friend, but it is true that people who hate themselves tend to repel rather than attract others.

If you are overweight, it's all right to diet. But it's not all right to starve yourself, a condition called anorexia. It's not all right to binge and then purge yourself (by vomiting or using laxatives), a condition called bulimia. Both these conditions are abnormal and require professional help.

The point is that even if you lose weight, you still have to learn how to make friends. Please note that most diets don't work and, more often than not, people soon gain back more than they originally lost. Most people overeat because they are anxious. They need to find alternative ways to reduce their anxiety. Instead of overeating, go for a walk, take a swim, exercise, do yoga, or try meditation.

Although it's not so much what you eat but what's eating you, you still have to cut down on foods that are high in fat and calories and low in nutritional value. You can eat a high volume of fruits, vegetables, pasta, and whole grains and still lose weight. By contrast, relatively small amounts of fatty goods and sweets can add extra pounds with little health benefit. Exercise also helps everyone become more fit.

Sometimes people worry about parts of their bodies for no rational reason. Some men worry about their penis size. But you can't tell the size of a penis by observing its non-erect state. Besides, the size of a penis is totally unrelated to sexual gratification. Some women think that their breasts are too small. Again, breast size has nothing to do with sexual pleasure. The popularity of small or large breasts with women seems to change with fashion. Some young men seem to have a "locker-room mentality" about breasts, but most of them grow out of this stage as they mature and begin to view women more as people than as objects of adolescent fantasy.

You can easily blame your appearance or some imagined physical "defect" for any problem you have, but that would be a cop-out. Why not focus instead on your personality, your generosity, and all the good qualities you possess that are not related to your looks?

THERE IS SOMEBODY FOR EVERYBODY
WHO FEELS REASONABLY GOOD
ABOUT HIMSELF OR HERSELF.
IF YOU HAVE AN INTEREST,
SOMEONE WILL BE INTERESTED IN YOU.
BUT IF YOU ARE BORED, YOU WILL BE
BORING TO BE WITH.

Are you bored or are you boring?

Everyone is bored now and then. That's of no particular significance. It's only when boredom becomes a way of life that you have to do something. There is nothing more uninteresting than a bunch of people standing around talking about how bored they are.

Here is a list of the most boring things you can do.

- Put yourself down. Tell yourself and others how worthless and rotten you are.
- Tell friends who ask how you feel all about your bad points.
- Tell people you're horny.
- Boast about things that everybody knows you haven't done.
- Watch more than two hours of TV a day. Have you noticed that the more you watch, the more bored you get?
- Constantly talk about only one subject (sports, sex, movies). It's okay to have one main interest, but if that's all you talk about, people will tune out.
- Always come across as a Pollyanna ("Oh, everything is wonderful!") or as a cynic ("Life stinks!").
- Relentlessly tell people how tired you are.
- Talk too much. You are not as boring if you talk too little, as long as you participate by listening.
- Be absolute about everything.
- Complain a lot.
- Be paranoid and suspicious about everyone's motives.
- Be overdependent on what other people think.
- Approach people by saying, "I don't want to trouble you, bore you, or take up too much of your time." That's fake humility.
- Be unwilling to try new experiences.

- Be a supermiser. You don't want to do interesting things because you "can't afford it." You don't know if you will ever be able to afford it.
- Persistently analyze other people's behavior and motives.
- Be a gossip.
- Nearly always wait to be asked and hardly ever do the asking.
- Be serious and humorless most of the time, or always kid around.
- Relieve your tension by using drugs or alcohol.
- Spoil other people's stories (because you've said, thought, or heard them before).
- Put on a slide show that lasts more than twenty minutes.
- Announce how self-sacrificing you are and what ungrateful slobs the other people around you are.
- Complain that there's nothing to do, or talk endlessly of plans for the future that usually don't pan out.
- Always insist on being the center of attention.

Being bored is very tiring. It's no accident that when employers want something done, they ask their busiest employee to do it. The more you do, the more alert you are and the more time you have to do all the things you want to do.

When you are bored, you also need to be especially careful about not taunting, tormenting, or hurting other people. Boredom is often one of the major causes of senseless delinquent acts and other evils.

The best medicine for overcoming boredom is to do or learn something new or different. This will give you a first-class rush, which can then motivate you to do or learn more.

You'll also become alert, energized, stimulated, and more confident. Now is the time to do things. It doesn't matter whether it's cleaning house, getting a ball game started, baking a cake, doing all the odd jobs you've been putting off, or finally starting a big project that you've been dreaming about.

While pulling yourself out of a bored state may seem difficult, if you are willing to take a chance and follow the suggestions listed below, you may not find it as hard as you originally thought it would be.

Go to the refrigerator or cupboard and eat or drink something with sugar in it. You'll feel better instantly, but the physical effect will last for only about two minutes. You probably will want to eat more but if you do, you might end up feeling worse than when you started. So here's the trick: Once you have eaten something sweet, begin doing something new or different right away. You have two minutes to start.

- Read an article that will give you some new information.
- Prepare a dish that you haven't made before and serve it to somebody.
- Buy something that you can't quite afford but for which you have been saving for a long time.
- Renew a friendship that you've neglected. Risk its working or not working out.
- Go to a charming place for a meal.
- Let someone close to you know that you are in a good mood.

Are you disabled or do you know someone who is?

If you yourself are not disabled in some way, you probably know someone who is. According to the American Coalition of Citizens with Disabilities, about thirty-six million Americans today—roughly one in six—suffer serious physical, mental, or emotional impairment.

Being disabled creates all kinds of difficulties—social, emotional, sexual, and, of course, economic. Part of the problem is that disabled people are often excluded from the mainstream of life by the rest of us.

As a psychologist who has worked with disabled people, I offer the following advice to people who are not disabled. Make an effort to befriend a disabled person. Do it with empathy and compassion. Form your friendship on the basis of a common interest or by helping the disabled person develop an interest in something that you already enjoy. Once you have established a relationship, don't treat the disabled person with exaggerated delicacy or sensitivity. In particular, don't hesitate to communicate your feelings. For example, you may find that your friend is misinterpreting your interest for love. If this is the case, the sooner you clear up the misunderstanding, the better.

The following is another important point: It's all right if you start out feeling uncomfortable. Very few people are initially fully comfortable in the company of someone who is blind, deaf, or has cerebral palsy. By acknowledging your discomfort, you can bypass feeling pity, shame, guilt, rejection, or the desire to withdraw. Talk about your discomfort so that your friend might be able to help you deal with it.

Here are a few "messages" to people with disabilities.

- No one can make you feel inferior without your consent.
- If you have interests, someone will be interested in you.
- If you are chronically bored, you will be boring company.
- If you have nothing to do, don't do it in the presence of others.
- Our society does not give you points for being disabled. You need to work hard to make friends and to prove to others that you are a person first and that your disability is secondary to everything that is important about you. *You* are not your disability.

Please note: If you know a child with a disability, read *One Miracle at a Time* by Irving Dickman and Sol Gordon (Fireside/Simon & Schuster, 1993, paperback).

You can't please everybody!

Are you the type who tries to please everybody?

Well, no one can. You can only *try* to keep your own life in order.

What pleases one friend, parent, or teacher may displease another. Your motives and actions are not always understood or appreciated. Therefore, the person that you need to satisfy most is yourself. By being your own person you'll find that some people, but not all (maybe not even many), will like you. Those people who try to please everybody end up pleasing nobody.

Why not just do the best you can? If your best isn't good enough for some people, that's their problem.

What really counts in relationships is intelligence, imagination, character, luck, and good will.

So you might as well get out and get to know some people.

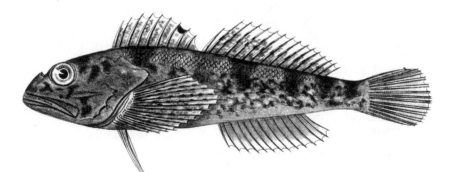

The legitimate purpose of anger is to make a grievance known. If that isn't done appropriately, anger can easily turn into hostility, a desire for revenge, or even violent rage.

Just blowing off steam often doesn't result in relief because it isn't considerate of the person at whom that anger is directed.

It is a good idea to count to ten before you express your anger, and sometimes it is a good idea to sit down and ask yourself, "Now whose problem is this?"

I agree with Carol Travis who says that if a person does not confront the object of a grievance, it matters little whether that person keeps anger in or lets it out. Those at whom rage is directed also have hurt feelings. Silent sulking, however, is the worst response to someone else's expressions of anger. It's a passive way of expressing hostility, which turns anger inward.

Try to avoid turning your anger into a total rejection of another person. Instead, stick to the issue. Don't say, "I hate you." Say, "I am angry about what you said or what you did."

Anger is a legitimate emotion. Violence, as Carolyn Swift suggests, is a response of weak, ineffective, inadequate people (villains) rather than of effective, strong, competent people (heroes, heroines).

If this situation has lasted a long time, and especially if you don't have friends to help you deal with it, you must do everything you can to put an end to it, even if you have to be dramatic and say you won't go to school anymore.

Tell your parents, teacher, principal, counselor, rabbi, or minister that you are afraid of being hurt and that it's up to them to intervene.

Sometimes the worst of this kind of behavior occurs in a particular place, such as the gym. Insist that something be done. Get a doctor's excuse if necessary. Nobody who attends a school should have to tolerate an unsafe situation.

It's a terrible feeling, and it gets much worse if you do nothing, sleep a lot, or just mope around. You might
- eat too much
- drink too much
- pace up and down
- do drugs
- watch too much television
- compare yourself with others

These actions don't fill the void. The only thing that can help is to face reality. This suggestion might make you very anxious, but take heart. The first sign of getting better is feeling anxious. It means that something *is* there, that you exist.

EMPTY NO LONGER.

You need to take care of yourself. Go for a walk, take a swim, or do another type of exercise. Try to connect with a friend whom you have neglected or a family member whom you haven't seen for some time, even if you think it won't help. Just keep on trying.

Talk about what's troubling you with a friend or some person whom you believe you can trust. Fill the void with ideas, alternatives, faith in the possibility that your circumstances can change. Prayer, if you are into it, can help.

You can begin to feel much better, even if nothing changes except that you have made an effort to fill the empty spaces.

Since the publication of the first edition of this book, I have received many letters from young people who wrote about their feelings of emptiness. I am reprinting one such letter and my response in the hope that they will help others with similar feelings.

Dear Dr. Gordon,

It is 11:04 P.M. and I am trying to fall asleep. I just finished reading your book because my older brother gave it to me off his shelf just 45 minutes ago after I had a talk with him about how I am feeling.

I am fourteen years old and I used to be happy. Just last year I was convinced that I had found myself and I was truly happy. I don't know if I can explain this. I have many friends, am smart in school, and am good at lots of things, but inside I am very unhappy. I don't know how long I've felt this way. It kind of just snuck up on me, but I know it's been around for at least three months.

The way I am is hard to explain. Everyone who knows me will say that I am so happy and I smile all the time. Many of my friends do not understand the emptiness I feel inside, like there's something out there but I don't quite know what I'm looking for. I feel unfulfilled, and though I am surrounded by friends constantly, I feel internally very lonely. I have thought about suicide, though for me it's not an option because I am trying to find life, not get rid of it. I am very confused and overwhelmed by life in general.

I am willing to just live this through if I know it will eventually end. I don't know if I could live with this forever. Maybe one day I will wake up and it will be gone. I hope so. Just taking time to read your book and write this letter has brought up my mood and opened me. Thank you. Please write back.

Susan

(Reprinted with permission from "Susan"—
not her real name.)

Dear Susan,

Since my book *When Living Hurts* was first published some years ago, I have received over one thousand letters from young people like you. For the most part, the letters fall into two categories: those that were sent by people (like you) who feel empty inside but are generally perceived by their friends to be happy and those that were sent by people who have been extremely disappointed by a failed love affair, uncertainty about their sexual orientation, or an inability to get along with their parents. In both instances the underlying problem is a basic depression that is revealed in many different ways. People who are disappointed, angry, or confused seem to be unable to separate unfortunate feelings or events from their whole personality. But failure is an event, not a person.

Feeling empty inside is a fairly common problem, and more often than not it is related to a false perception of what life is supposed to be like. Often people like you are seeking the "meaning of life" and don't understand that life is an opportunity, not a meaning. One must enjoy and appreciate the opportunities one has now, at the same time making plans and being hopeful about the future. Things do change and improve (even after a terrible loss, like a death in the family), but this doesn't happen spontaneously, like waking up one morning and finding that everything is fine.

Changes in one's life almost always require a lot of effort and patience. The best way to effect change in your life is to go outside yourself in a sense—to do good deeds and be helpful to others. This is called "mitzvah therapy" because while you are being nice to others, you are also helping yourself. It's amazing how acts of kindness can transform a life. Even just being nice to a person who is lonely, is being picked on, or has no friends can make a big difference in your life. Another way to cope with internal depression is to learn something new. It doesn't matter what it is—learning a new language, a craft, chess or simply becoming acquainted with a particular author's work. I do recommend that for more suggestions you read my book *The Teenage Survival Book* (Random House, 1988). If that book doesn't help you, then I recommend you seek counseling to explore some of the inner conflicts that you might be experiencing.

One final note of caution: Approximately ten percent of the cases of depression have some physical cause. If you often find yourself depressed for no apparent reason, it would be a good idea to get a complete physical examination and tell your doctor about the way you feel. If for any reason the doctor tries to trivialize what you say or makes you feel that you don't know what is going on inside you, he or she is not the right physician for you, and you should look for another.

With best wishes for your personal growth.

Sol Gordon

Did something terrible happen to you when you were a child?

Although we like to think that children are resilient and flexible, some individuals experience childhood abuse or trauma that causes stress, guilt, or anxiety in later years.

If someone you cared about took advantage of you sexually, the first thing you have to remember is that it wasn't your fault regardless of the circumstances—even if you didn't tell anyone or you agreed to or liked the act. All mental health specialists agree that when an adult commits such an act, it's never the child's responsibility or fault.

Or maybe you did something wrong. Maybe you made a mistake. But now it's done. Why continue to punish yourself? The best thing to do is to admit your mistakes and talk about them with someone you trust. Then try to be helpful to others who have had similar experiences.

If you had bad thoughts and something happened soon after, remember that your bad thoughts didn't cause that thing to happen. Your thoughts cannot make accidents happen or bring about natural events (like death).

Getting on with your life will not only help you but also those you care about. If you cannot get over your upset or depression, talking about your feelings with a trusted family member, friend, rabbi, counselor, or minister might help you gain a more positive perspective. Sometimes just being understood by someone else is enough to help a person begin developing new attitudes.

Life does not exist without disappointments, upsets, accidents, tragedies, and loss.

What was the worst thing that ever happened to you?

Did you learn anything from the experience that could help you now or in the future?

Stop and look at some situations that seem negative or painful. Look at each one from a different angle, as though you were turning a diamond over and over in your hand, examining all its facets.

Remember: Every mistake can become a lesson. Even tragic events can become lessons. The ghosts of the past don't have to determine what you can do today.

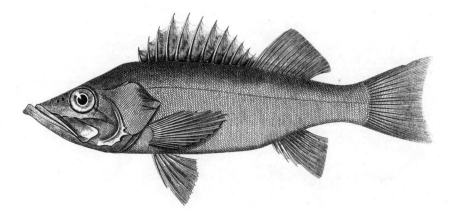

Do most people fall short of your expectations?

Is it possible that your standards are too high? Unrealistic? Unrealizable? Unreasonable expectations are the main reasons that
- so many marriages end in divorce
- so many parents are angry with their children
- so many children are disappointed in their parents
- so many love affairs break up

Think about the following:

WE ALL HAVE OUR LIMITATIONS.

YOU ARE NOT YOUR THOUGHTS.
YOU ARE WHAT YOU DO.

At times you can get some insights about yourself by examining your thoughts, dreams, and fantasies.

You can use your imagination to write poems and love letters.

BUT ONLY WHAT YOU DO WITH YOUR
THOUGHTS DETERMINES WHO YOU ARE.

Remember, *all* thoughts, turn-ons, fantasies, and dreams are normal. They could come to you voluntarily or involuntarily from your unconscious. Although some of them are subject to your control, most are not.

Guilt is the energy for the involuntary repetition of unacceptable thoughts.

If you recognize this, then it doesn't matter how weird or frightening your thoughts are. You will realize that it is normal to have violent thoughts, such as imagining that your friends are dead. You will accept that it is normal to imagine having sex with someone you're not supposed to have sex with. Your thoughts will pass and nothing will happen. Your thoughts will not control you.

But if you allow your thoughts to paralyze you or if you permit them to lead you to violent actions, then your thoughts are not responsible for the outcomes. You are!

If you say you can't help having these agonizing thoughts, it may be because you have not yet realized that thoughts of all kinds are normal. Thoughts become abnormal only

• when they take up most of your time

- if you respond to them with compulsive or impulsive behavior
- when they are repressed and then emerge in the form of fears and psychosomatic disorders

If you want to know more about rational thinking, I recommend that you read *How to Stubbornly Refuse to Make Yourself Miserable about Anything . . . Yes, Anything* by Albert Ellis (Lyle Stuart, Inc., 1988).

It's possible that just by reading this section, you'll feel greatly relieved. Remember the Zen expression, "When the mind is ready, a teacher appears." It is also possible for a bad situation that has lasted for years to change in minutes. Many people have experienced this. It usually is the result of an insight, a love affair, or doing something useful. This may not be happening to you right now, but remember that it can happen.

If it has reached the point that your thoughts have become painful, seek help from a counselor, therapist, or clergy person.

2

If You or Someone You Know Is Suicidal

How to get help urgently

It's important to understand that depression can distort your thinking. You may feel stupid even if you have a high IQ. You may feel alone even though you have friends and people who care about you. You may feel empty even if you have dreams and plans. You may feel that nothing can change even though you've been in tough spots before and things did change for the better.

Tell someone you trust that you are depressed and need help. And promise that person you won't harm yourself (even though you've had suicidal thoughts) because you want to give "help" another chance.

After reading this part of the book and any other sections that pertain to your situation, confide in someone about what's troubling you, even if you have to reach out to several people before you get the response that helps you feel better. Speak to a friend or a parent first, even if you doubt that person will understand. Then confide in a trustworthy doctor, counselor, teacher, minister, rabbi, or call a crisis intervention center anytime day or night. Someone there will help you.

If it's someone you know who is in trouble—perhaps

someone whom you care about has confided in you—turn immediately to the section "What to do if someone you care about is suicidal (page 45). Then read "Dying to live the good life?" (page 43).

If you feel that the danger of suicide is imminent, don't leave the person alone. If possible you or another person should call the police or a suicide prevention hot line and report that a suicide attempt is in progress. Make sure you give the address and telephone number. Get as close to the person as he or she will allow and say, "Let's talk. For my sake. It's important to me. If I can't persuade you not to kill yourself, you can go ahead with it later. Please, let's talk. It's possible that I don't understand how you feel. Explain it to me." Try to get the person to discuss possible options and alternatives.

HANDS

i think of my poems and songs
as hands
if i don't hold them out to you
afraid that you might
laugh at them
spit on them
or totally ignore them
i find i won't be touched

if i keep them in my pocket
i will never get to see you
seeing me
seeing you

and though i know
from experience
many of you
for a myriad of reasons
will laugh
and spit
and walk away unmoved
still
to meet those of you
who do reach out
is well worth the risk
and pain

so
here are my hands
do what you will
—Walt Whitman

How to help someone who is in a panic or having what's sometimes called an anxiety attack

Anxiety is experienced as an overwhelming state of tension or fear (often the result of the anticipation of some unknown danger or of not being able to handle a scheduled task or performance), which should not be confused with normal stress or tension before an event. Anxiety attacks may be accompanied by certain physical reactions, such as a rapid heartbeat, sweating, trembling, nausea, difficulty with normal breathing,* in addition to intense fears of losing control, going crazy, and even dying.

Here's what to do when someone is having such an attack. Say something like "Listen, you are having an anxiety attack. If you've had one before, you know you'll get over it. If it's the first time, it's very scary. But it is not dangerous and it will pass. [How do you know? the person asks.] I read about it in a book. [What causes it?] It's not important to discuss that now.

"Here's what you are supposed to do. Sit down, close your eyes, and tense up. Then relax every part of your body. Start with your toes, feet, legs . . . . " (Progressively name the other body parts and suggest that the person visualize those body parts in his or her mind.)

"I'll stay with you. I know that all kinds of ideas will come into your mind. This is common. It happens to a lot of people. [How do you know?] It was clearly stated in a psychology book that I read. What you are going through is not comfortable and may even be terrifying, but it is *not*, I repeat, *not* dangerous."

---

*If the person is panting and out of breath, one way to help him or her breathe normally is to have the person place a small paper bag around the nose and mouth and breathe into the bag until the panting stops. Breathing the same air over and over for three or four minutes helps the person control the panting by restoring the carbon dioxide in the blood to normal levels, calming the person down.

Stay as calm as you can for your own sake and your friend's. It's okay to be scared in a crisis. Just know your limits and know when to get help.

Please note: This is a first-aid procedure. Don't try to talk a person out of the anxiety attack by suggesting that it's nothing to worry about. Nor will the relaxation approach solve the basic problem. If intense physical pain is present, emergency medical help may be needed. If it does turn out to be, as you suspected, an anxiety attack, suggest that the person talk with a counselor or psychiatrist at a later time.

When the acute phase of the attack is over, the two of you could decide what to do now and what to postpone for a later time.

KNOWING WHAT TO DO
TO HELP SOMEONE IN TROUBLE
IS A GOOD FEELING.

Are you sometimes depressed? *Everybody* gets depressed occasionally. Almost all such depressions are normal. Have you ever thought about suicide? Did you know that almost everyone has?

Do you know someone who has killed himself or herself? Isn't it painful to recall or visualize that person? Wouldn't you like to be in a position to help someone (perhaps even yourself) who is seriously considering committing suicide?

People who think about or actually commit suicide in response to feeling depressed have not learned how to deal with disappointment. They feel that there is no way out of their situation or that their agony will last forever. They feel that no one believes in or understands them. For them, life is no longer meaningful. Many of these people haven't grasped the fact that life without frustrations, depressions, and profound periods of mourning simply doesn't exist. But mostly they find it inconceivable to imagine that

- things can always change
- they have many options

Many experts claim they can tell if a person is suicidal, but they can't. Every person is unique, as are the reasons for suicide. What we can say with certainty is that every suicidal statement of intent is a cry for help, as is every suicide attempt.

Anyone who is suicidal requires professional help and, sometimes, antidepressant medication. But psychiatrists, psychologists, and social workers can't "cure" a depressed person without the help of that person's friends and family.

The following is a bit of personal philosophy of life that I have found can be helpful.

- Don't go around looking for *the* meaning of life. Look for an opportunity to have meaningful experiences.
- Disappointments are a part of everybody's life.
- If you don't expect miracles to occur in your life, you won't notice them when they happen.
- The first miracle takes place when you stop comparing yourself to others.

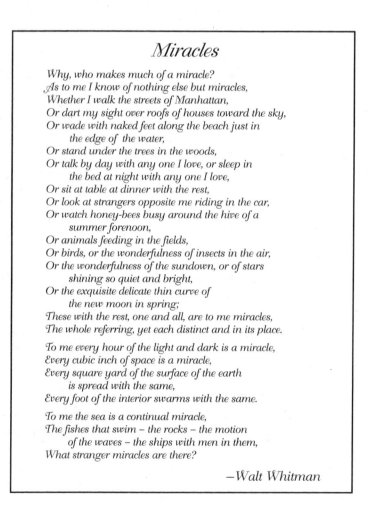

Miracles

Why, who makes much of a miracle?
As to me I know of nothing else but miracles,
Whether I walk the streets of Manhattan,
Or dart my sight over roofs of houses toward the sky,
Or wade with naked feet along the beach just in
    the edge of the water,
Or stand under the trees in the woods,
Or talk by day with any one I love, or sleep in
    the bed at night with any one I love,
Or sit at table at dinner with the rest,
Or look at strangers opposite me riding in the car,
Or watch honey-bees busy around the hive of a
    summer forenoon,
Or animals feeding in the fields,
Or birds, or the wonderfulness of insects in the air,
Or the wonderfulness of the sundown, or of stars
    shining so quiet and bright,
Or the exquisite delicate thin curve of
    the new moon in spring;
These with the rest, one and all, are to me miracles,
The whole referring, yet each distinct and in its place.

To me every hour of the light and dark is a miracle,
Every cubic inch of space is a miracle,
Every square yard of the surface of the earth
    is spread with the same,
Every foot of the interior swarms with the same.

To me the sea is a continual miracle,
The fishes that swim – the rocks – the motion
    of the waves – the ships with men in them,
What stranger miracles are there?

—Walt Whitman

Listen to that person. Don't argue or attempt to prove that what he or she is planning to do doesn't make sense. Respond by saying things like:
- It must be so painful for you.
- As long as you are alive, things can change.
- I'll help and always stick by you.
- I care about you.

Don't say:
- You're being silly (*or* stupid).
- Let's forget about it.
- Let's have some fun.
- Let's go to a movie or a dance.

Don't suggest taking a drink or drugs. Lowering inhibitions and muddying thinking can make a person reckless and can possibly lead to suicide.

Don't be afraid to talk with your friend or brother or sister about what he or she is thinking or planning to do. You might ask, "Have you ever felt as though life's not worth living?" You will not be putting ideas into the person's head. On the contrary, if the person is considering suicide, it's good for him or her to talk about it. *Direct questions about suicidal intent do not provoke suicidal behavior.* Ask the person: "Have you ever wished you were dead?" "Are you thinking of suicide?" "Are there some things you've thought about or done that you've never told anyone?" Then find out how urgent the crisis is. Ask: "How do you plan to kill yourself?" "Have you been thinking about dying for some time now?" "When do you think you'll kill yourself?"

If the crisis is urgent (if the person knows how he or she

plans to die, has the means, and is ready to act), *do not leave the person.* Take him or her to a parent, a counselor, a minister, a rabbi, a suicide prevention clinic, or whatever support system seems best at the time. If the person refuses to meet with anyone, secretly call someone for help. *Try not to bear the burden of the responsibility alone.*

Any expressed suicidal intent or inference should be taken seriously. Inferences might include comments like:

- I won't be around much longer.
- Soon nobody will have to worry about me.
- I have nothing to live for.
- Nothing works for me.
- I'm a loser.

If the expressions of suicide seem serious but not urgent, talk with the person and really listen to find out what's troubling him or her.

Usually something has happened in that person's life to cause a serious crisis. Among the possibilities are rejection by a lover, the death of a close family member, an impending divorce, or the loss of employment.

It doesn't matter if *you* think what the person is upset about is trivial. It's how the person feels that counts.

Accept the feelings that are being expressed. Don't tell the person not to worry. Don't minimize the event by saying things like "You'll get over it" or "It's nothing" or "You think you have troubles?" Don't try to coax the person out of the hurt he or she feels.

Do

- be a friend and empathize
- be sad with the person
- give the person a hug
- take the person for a walk
- jog together
- exercise together

Stay with the person as long as possible. Make a definite appointment for your next visit. Say: "Call me anytime—even in the middle of the night." Go out for a meal or an ice cream. The act of sharing a meal can lift depression, if only for a short time. Make a pact with your friend—what he or she will do, what you will do, when you will meet—and compare notes. Let your friend know you will see him or her through this.

Show that you care. Everybody needs someone who believes in him or her.

Don't

- take the person to parties or anyplace where people are having fun. (Most really sad people become even more depressed when they are around people who are having a good time.)
- try to give easy answers or solve the person's problems for him or her.
- ask your friend, "Is this the worst thing that's ever happened?"
- tell lies like "She (he) really does love you" or "Everybody is your friend."
- put the person on a heavy guilt or religious trip.

Don't say things like "You have everything going for you." Instead, respond with such caring messages as "If you think I don't know how you feel, tell me more so I can understand better."

And tell your friend how much you would feel the loss of his or her presence in your life. The main thing is for you to encourage your friend to talk, reveal his or her thoughts, and confide in you.

Doctors can help in dealing with depressions. In some crisis situations medication can result in almost immediate relief. What doesn't work is a response that reveals blame, resentment, or hostility.

Earl A. Grollman cautions in his excellent book *Suicide* that the suicidal person is already suffering from a burden of "punishing guilt feelings." If that person is told by society and religion that suicide is immoral, his or her guilt and depression may increase. For the suicidal person, Grollman says, suicide isn't a theological issue but the result of terrible emotional stress. The main thing is for you to encourage your friend to talk, reveal his or her thoughts, and confide in you.

Nobody ever fully recovers from the death of a child, a close friend, or a sibling who commits suicide. It is difficult not to be haunted by a dreadful sense of having done something wrong or of having failed to do something right.

So many people who commit, try to commit, or even think about suicide do so because they feel a sense of hopelessness and sometimes a sense that life is without purpose or meaning. They may feel that threatening to kill themselves is heroic.

But it is not heroic. It shows a failure to connect meaningfully with people who might or would like to love and believe in them.

Do not keep a suicidal intent confidential

If you are told in confidence that someone you care about is considering suicide, do you tell anyone? Yes!

Find a way to tell a person's parents, spouse, counselor, minister, or rabbi that you are worried. The more worried you are, the more explicit you should be.

This is not easy. Sometimes the best you can do isn't good enough. You can't always trust your own judgment about whether the threat of suicide is serious or not.

You could easily be thinking that
- the person is not the type
- the person is carrying on or is just using suicide as an attention-getting device
- you don't believe the person is serious
- the person seems much better now

Many people commit suicide after their depression has lifted and they have regained the energy to go through with the suicide. A person may have already decided to commit suicide and, therefore, comes across as very calm, as if she or he has nothing more to worry about. *This calm period is a dangerous time and is a signal.*

If your friend refuses to get help, you might start by calling a crisis center. Give your friend this book to read. Encourage him or her to talk to another close friend or relative.

Please realize that nobody expects you to be the therapist and resolve the problem. At the same time you may be the only person your friend confides in and, therefore, the only person who can help. By determining the seriousness of the crisis, motivating the person to seek help, and showing your support, you can make a difference.

If the person says to you, "Leave me alone," you should be aware that he or she seldom means it.

THE CRUCIAL POINT FOR YOU
TO UNDERSTAND IS THAT
SUICIDAL INTENT IS ALWAYS TEMPORARY.
IT CAN BE REVERSED.

Can you tell the difference between a cry for help, a wish for attention, and depression?

You can't always, but here are some points to consider.

Francine Klagsbrun, in her excellent book for parents and counselors titled *Too Young to Die—Youth and Suicide*, writes:

> Friends, relatives, teachers, coworkers . . . make up the front line of defense against suicide. . . . And they must help, even if they believe the suicidal person is manipulating them or using threats of suicide to gain attention. A person who must resort to suicide to get attention has lost the ability to communicate in normal ways. *The person needs attention* [Emphasis added]. Without it the next cry for help will be shriller, more desperate, more dangerous.

Erring on the side of concern is better than being sorry later.

There are two main kinds of suicide: the impulsive kind that ends a life and the slow, not entirely intentional kind that often produces equally grim results. The second kind may include:
- Driving while intoxicated
- Drug addiction
- Alcoholism
- Fasting
- Eating too much (especially if self-induced vomiting follows a binge)
- Smoking
- Suicide attempts
- Sexual promiscuity
- Violence and crime
- Retreating into despair

The signs could also indicate depression, extreme anxiety, physical illness, or a temporary, and even an appropriate, response to loss. They include:

- The expression of feelings of hopelessness
- Incommunicative behavior
- Explosive outbursts
- A loss of appetite or excessive eating
- A loss of interest in activities once considered enjoyable
- A loss of energy or extreme fatigue
- Relentless pacing
- Sleeplessness
- A preoccupation with the notion that "nobody understands"
- Talk about death or suicide
- Moodiness and sudden bursts of crying
- Increased isolation from friends and family
- A tendency to become more active and aggressive than usual (unlike suicidal adults, who tend to become apathetic when severely depressed)
- A serious drop in grades for those still in school or college
- The giving away of valued possessions
- An increased interest in getting his or her "life in order"
- A sudden and intense interest in religious beliefs and the afterlife
- A profound depression in response to a recent loss, such as a divorce or death in the family or a close friend's moving away
- A previous suicide attempt

Even though the vast majority of people who exhibit one or more of the above signs will not attempt or commit suicide or become mentally ill, these signs do represent, for the most part, *changes* in behavior that warrant serious concern.

Here is something to think about:

> In some cases you may find yourself in the position of having to get direct help for someone who is suicidal and refuses to go for counseling. If so, do it. Don't be afraid of appearing disloyal. Many people who are suicidal have given up hope. They no longer believe they can be helped. They feel it is useless. The truth is, they can be helped. With time, most suicidal people can be restored to full and happy living. But when they are feeling hopeless, their judgment is impaired. They can't see a reason to go on living. In that case, it is up to you to use your judgment to see that they get the help they need. What at the time may appear to be an act of disloyalty or the breaking of a confidence could turn out to be the favor of a lifetime. Your courage and willingness to act could save a life.
>
> Excerpted from *Suicide in Youth and What You Can Do about It.* Prepared by the Suicide Prevention and Crisis Center of San Mateo County, California, in cooperation with the American Association of Suicidology and Merck Sharp & Dohme

---

"Whoever preserves one life, it is as if he preserved an entire world."
—Talmud

Why are so many young people killing themselves?

We don't really know. We do know that the suicide rate among young people between the ages of fifteen and twenty-four has tripled in the past thirty years, resulting in between five thousand and six thousand deaths a year. In addition, several hundred thousand young people make serious suicide attempts every year. We do know that many of the suicides are the children of parents who have divorced or separated. But thirteen million children under eighteen have divorced parents. Other reasons that experts give for the suicide rate among young people are:

- Not getting along with parents
- Drug and alcohol abuse
- Feeling depressed by the loss of a parent or friend
- Feeling useless
- Feeling unloved and unlovable
- Being rejected by a girlfriend or boyfriend
- Fears that are related to sex

Most experts agree that the following are characteristics of suicide:

- Depression or a feeling of hopelessness is the most important cause of suicide.
- Almost all suicides are preventable.
- Many people who took their own lives had made it known in some way that they were intending to do so. Suicide attempts of any kind should always be considered a "cry for help."
- Almost all suicidal people have mixed feelings about the act: They want to do it and they don't. Suicide is sometimes impulsive, but it may also be an act of desperation or the result of a desire for revenge.

- People who kill themselves often feel that their families don't understand them. Their suicide usually is the culmination of a long period of multiple difficulties (and the result of the ready availability of a gun).

However intolerable the emotion or unendurable the pain, it will pass. It will change. It's temporary. As long as the person is alive, there is time for everything, including figuring out why he or she wanted to die.

Research by Jan Alan Fawcett, M.D. (Professor of Psychiatry, Rush Presbyterian St. Luke's Medical Center) suggests that symptoms like severe anxiety, panic attacks,* diminished concentration, and profound loss of interest or ability to experience pleasure seem to be significant predictors of the early onset of suicide attempts. Dr. Fawcett makes a special point of stating that severe anxiety and other related symptoms can be alleviated if they are recognized and treated.

WHY DO SO MANY YOUNG PEOPLE
WANT TO END IT ALL?
WHAT'S THE RUSH?
THEY'VE GOT A WHOLE LIFETIME
AHEAD OF THEM.

In addition to the factors related to depression, many suicidal people haven't learned how to cope with disappointment. We live in a society that values instant gratification. When people feel bad, they often take a pill or a drink or do something to try to escape how they feel. If they can't get relief right away, they may be overcome by despair. Everybody has to learn to cope with disappoint-

---

*Common symptoms of panic attacks that may appear without apparent cause are shortness of breath, dizziness, heart palpitations, trembling, sweating, nausea, hot flashes or chills, terror, fear of going crazy or losing control, and fear of dying.

ments and even tragic happenings. That's part of living. A bad situation does not always resolve itself as quickly as we would like, and it's easy to become discouraged. However, everything does eventually change, especially if we work at it. If someone we love doesn't understand this, it's up to us to convince that person. There is no greater mitzvah* than to save a life.

---

*"Although the world is full of suffering,
it is also full of the overcoming of it."*
—Helen Keller

John Dunſtall *fecit*.   P. Stent *excu*.

Mitzvah is a Hebrew word that means a "commandment" but is usually translated as a "good deed."

56 ·

Are you dying to be the center of attention?

What's the point of being the center of attention if you are dead? You'll never know about it.

If you think that the only way to get your parents to listen to you is to make a suicide attempt, you should think again. You might actually die or botch up the job, leaving you disfigured and disabled.

Attempting suicide is just not a good way to get attention. Suicide is romantic in novels. In real life it's a horror.

What if you think that life isn't worth living?

You may not know whether life is worth living or not until you've lived at least half of yours. When you will be forty, you will be able to reexamine what has happened to you. Then you can ask yourself the ultimate question: Has it been worth it?

Strange as it may seem to you now, in almost all cases people answer yes.

Whatever age you are, living requires courage.

"Courage is the ability to dispose of self-pity and wallowing. You have to look beyond yourself. Courage is not, in any way, self-centered *except* it is self-confident. The courageous person says, 'It's okay. I can beat this.' "
—Monica Dickens

Please read the following special appeal from a bereaved mother.

Please Promise Me
That You Won't Do Anything
to Hurt Yourself

I spoke with one of the leading suicide researchers in the country about two weeks before my son decided to take his own life. He told me that the most important intervention for severely depressed persons was to get them to promise not to do anything to hurt themselves. I didn't use that intervention with my son because I was totally unaware that he might become suicidal. So that my son may not have totally died in vain, I am asking *you* to please promise me that *you* won't do anything to hurt yourself. It is depression that is distorting your thinking. My son wrote that he was stupid at a time when he was being elected to Phi Beta Kappa. My son said he was lonely, that he had alienated almost everyone. My son was revered by many. Depression brings distorted thinking.

My son was a kind, concerned, and thoughtful person. I can't believe that he would have wanted to cause pain to so many people. He wouldn't have wanted to spoil graduation for his housemates or his girlfriend. My son said he felt guilty about the cost of his education and the sacrifice that it entailed. Not graduating, not fulfilling any promise after graduation was certainly not a rational solution to irrational guilt. I'm sure my son would not have wanted any one of thousands of ordinary situations to cause me remorse and pain—searing, sharp, horrid pain. I'm sure that my son would not have wanted to destroy elderly and sick grandparents. My son made a grievous error. You can make a better choice. *Please, please promise me that you won't do anything to hurt yourself or anyone else by rash impulse or distorted thought.* If I sound desperate, I am. I can't imagine that my sensitive, accomplished son would have wanted to harm his friends and family.

Help and relief will eventually come. A friend of my son had a major depression. She tried to hurt herself and failed. She got treatment. She is now well. It might take time, but you will get well, too. In the meantime, your promising not to hurt yourself is the only consolation I can have. Please help to console me. Promise that if you have out-of-control feelings, you'll call 911 or call a hospital. Right now, find someone to call, and write that number down. Put it where you can easily find it at any time. I know the world is full of answering machines. But if you plan now, you can help to save yourself if the need arises. Remember, I am counting on it. Thank you.

Author's note: In case it's not absolutely clear from the above letter, medical management of depression should begin as soon as symptoms are apparent.

Suggestions for survivors by Iris Bolton

My deep concern for young people who are experiencing suicidal thoughts prompts me to include the following suggestions from parents and friends of people who committed suicide, taken from Iris Bolton's book *My Son . . . My Son: A Guide to Healing after Death, Loss, or Suicide* (Bolton Press). The suggestions may help you decide to get help. If your concern is for someone else, the insights of these survivors might assist you in determining the best way to help that person.

- Know that you can survive. You may not think so but you can.
- Struggle with why it happened until you no longer need to know why or until you are satisfied with partial answers.
- Know that you may feel overwhelmed by the intensity of your feelings but all your feelings are normal.
- Anger, guilt, confusion, and forgetfulness are common responses. You are not crazy. You are in mourning.
- Be aware that you may feel appropriate anger at the person, at the world, at God, at yourself. It's okay to express your feelings.
- You may feel guilty for what you think you did or did not do. Guilt can turn into regret, through forgiveness.
- Having suicidal thoughts is common. It does not mean that you will act on those thoughts.
- Remember to take one moment or one day at a time.
- Find a good listener with whom you can share your thoughts. Call someone if you need to talk.
- Don't be afraid to cry. Tears are healing.
- Give yourself time to heal.

- Remember, the choice was not yours. No one is the sole influence in another's life.
- Expect setbacks. If emotions return like a tidal wave, you may only be experiencing a remnant of grief, an unfinished piece.
- Try to put off major decisions.
- Give yourself permission to get professional help.
- Be aware of the pain of your family and friends.
- Be patient with yourself and with others who may not understand.
- Set your own limits and learn to say no.
- Steer clear of people who want to tell you *what* or *how* to feel.
- Know there are support groups that can be helpful, such as Compassionate Friends or Survivors of Suicide groups. If not, ask a professional to help start one.
- Call on your personal faith to help you through.
- It is common to experience physical reactions to your grief, e.g., headaches, loss of appetite, inability to sleep.
- The willingness to laugh with others and at yourself is healing.
- Wear out your questions, anger, guilt, or other feelings until you can let them go. Letting go doesn't mean forgetting.
- Know that you will never be the same again but you can survive and even go beyond just surviving.

3

Sex and Love
Worries and Facts

This section is written mainly for teenagers and young adults but everyone, especially parents, can profit from it.

Are you worried about sex?

I don't think teenagers should have sexual intercourse. They are too young, too vulnerable, too easily exploitable. Ninety percent of teenagers don't use contraceptives the first time they have sex. They don't realize that a person's first experience of sex is usually grim. (Seldom does a girl have an orgasm; a boy gets his three days later when he tells the guys about it.) But if you are going to have sex anyway, use protection. It's not romantic to let it just happen. It's stupid.

AIDS alert and STD* cautions
(*sexually transmitted disease)

AIDS (Acquired Immunodeficiency Syndrome) is the late stage of an infection caused by HIV (Human Immunodeficiency Virus). This virus damages the immune system, leaving a person susceptible to infections and some cancers. As of this writing, AIDS is a fatal disease.

It could take as long as ten years before a person infected with the virus acquires AIDS. It does appear that not everyone with an HIV-positive diagnosis will develop full-blown AIDS, but everyone who is positive can infect other people by engaging in unprotected sex or sharing unclean needles, like those used for injecting drugs. Infected women who become pregnant can also pass on the virus to their babies.

HIV is mainly transmitted by sexual contact. In the United States and Canada it has mostly affected gay and bisexual men who have engaged in anal intercourse. Now it is spreading rapidly through heterosexual intercourse. In many countries of the world, especially those in Asia and Africa, the disease is spread primarily through heterosexual intercourse. In the United States currently one out of five people with AIDS is in his or her twenties. These people were probably exposed to the virus in their teens. (Source: National Adolescent Student Health Survey, American School Health Association, 1987)

HIV organisms are usually found in semen, vaginal fluids, and the blood of infected people.

Unless both people in a sexual relationship (regardless of sexual orientation) are monogymous, honest, and absolutely certain about the other's sexual history, the practice of safer sex is essential. This includes the use of latex condoms with a spermicide containing Nonoxynol-9 and the avoidance of anal and oral sex. Sex with multiple partners or prostitutes should also be avoided. In order for the virus to spread, there must be transmission of bodily fluids (that is, semen, vaginal fluids, and/or blood), so don't let such fluids enter your body. Even safer sex is not 100 percent safe. Deep kissing, sexual massage, and mutual masturbation fall into the category of safer sex. HIV is not transmitted by casual contact, like holding hands and hugging.

If you are concerned about being at risk, get an HIV antibody test. Any health department will inform you about the location of confidential testing sites. For an accurate reading you should wait at least eight weeks after your last possible exposure to the virus and be retested as often as health care providers suggest. If you prove to be HIV positive, you *must* seek medical guidance, and counseling is highly recommended. You must also take care of yourself so that you will be around when the cure is found. Be sure to inform all sexual partners, past and present, about your condition.

What are the symptoms of AIDS?

At first AIDS symptoms can resemble common illnesses such as colds and stomach flu. Some of the symptoms are:
- persistent or chronic diarrhea
- fever, chills, or night sweats
- extreme weight loss
- swollen glands on the neck or under the arms
- purple, pink, or brown spots on the body
- white spots or sores in the mouth
- a dry cough or shortness of breath
- memory loss or confusion

If you have any of these or other unusual symptoms, consult a doctor or a nurse who knows about AIDS. If you don't know where to go, call your local hot line. The AIDS hot line number is 1-800-342-AIDS. Also read *What You Can Do to Avoid AIDS* by Ervin "Magic" Johnson (Times Books, 1992).

It is not only AIDS or an unwanted pregnancy that you have to worry about. Nor is it only the sexually transmitted diseases you hear about most, like syphilis (about 120,000 cases annually) or gonorrhea (about 1,100,000 cases annually). Do you know about chlamydia (about 4 million cases each year)? Almost half of these people do not have initial symptoms, but if the disease is left untreated, it can cause sterility. There is also PID (Pelvic Inflammatory Disease)—420,000 cases—and genital herpes—500,000 cases (still without a cure and hard to diagnose in women). Also "going around" are genital warts and hepatitis B (for which there is an immunization, but only about 10 percent of sexually active people bother to be immunized). A recent report in the *New York Times* (April 1, 1993) concluded that 12 million new sexually transmitted infections occur each year, two-thirds of them contracted by people under 25 and one quarter by teenagers.

So don't have sex without a condom *and* a female form of birth control. If the male partner says he feels nothing when he uses a condom, the female partner should reply, "Then you won't get any feelings at all from me."

Sexual fantasies

All thoughts, wishes, dreams, fantasies, sexual turn-ons, no matter how weird, are normal. Often these feelings come from the primitive unconscious, and we have no control over them. If you recognize this fact, such thoughts of yours will pass and nothing will happen. If you feel guilty about your fantasies, they will probably recur. *Remember, guilt is the energy that fuels the repetition of unacceptable ideas.* They could become obsessive and cause unacceptable behavior. Remember, all sexual thoughts and turn-ons are okay, but not exploitive behavior. It's all right to think about sexual seduction, but it's not acceptable to exploit someone.

Of course, the ultimate fantasy is to fall in love with someone whose fantasy is to fall in love with you. This sometimes happens in reality. The ultimate turn-on is getting to know, trust, and become intimate with someone you love.

Masturbation is a healthy, normal expression of sexuality for both males and females. It is not physically harmful no matter how frequently you do it. (Males do not use up their supply of sperm, which is replenished and available all their lives.) A person can, however, live a healthy, normal life without ever having masturbated. If you feel guilty about masturbation or if you don't like it, don't do it. But it's normal. Almost all males and most females masturbate.

Voluntary behavior is the best kind. For example, eating is normal, but if people eat too much because they are anxious (and not because they are hungry), eating becomes involuntary (compulsive). The same is true of drinking alcohol. If you must have a compulsion, choose masturbation. Compulsive eating and alcoholism (compulsive drinking) can do your body great harm, but nobody has ever died of overmasturbating.

Dying for a fake orgasm?

Some young people have been experimenting with putting a rope around their neck and masturbating, falsely believing that they can get great orgasms in that way. Not true. Although a person might get a pleasurable sensation for a second or two in that way, most people don't realize how easy it is to lose consciousness. Sometimes just turning the wrong way will cause loss of consciousness and/or death.

Some teenagers have been experimenting with butyl nitrite (sold under such labels as "Rush," "Thrust," "Heart On," or "Hardware"). Although butyl nitrite might give a person a thirty second high, it can also cause a dizzy spell, blacking out, an irregular heartbeat, and permanent damage to brain tissue. Butyl nitrite in combination with drugs such as alcohol is even more deadly. More than a few teenagers have died for the sake of a rush that lasts half a minute! LSD can also send you on a trip from which you'll never recover. It is a dangerous drug.

Really great orgasms can be achieved by masturbating (and fantasizing at the same time), if you do so without guilt. Masturbation can be relaxing and has no harmful side effects. But if you feel guilty about masturbating, you'll find that you will increase tension instead of reducing it. If you have an impulse to hurt or exploit someone or yourself in a sexual way, masturbate instead (privately, creatively, and with lubrication), and you'll be surprised how quickly your impulse will disappear. The impulse may reappear, but you now know what to do about it. If masturbation bothers you or you feel that you are not in control, get counseling.

We don't know why certain people are homosexual, but we do know that homosexuality is *not* a disease or a disorder. Recent clinical evidence suggests that some people are born homosexual. Some scientists think it is a trait that develops very early in life. Others maintain that both a genetic predisposition and early development play a role in a human being's sexual identity. Some people say they knew that they were homosexual at a very early age. Sexual orientation by its very nature cannot be taught, nor can a person's appearance convey whether he or she is homosexual. Effeminacy in males and masculinity in females are not necessarily characteristics of homosexuality. Most gay men are not effeminate, and most lesbians are not masculine.

The majority of intelligent and sexually mature people are aware that they have both homosexual and heterosexual thoughts and feelings at some times during their lives and that these are quite normal occurrences. Childhood and adolescent attraction to members of one's own sex are not uncommon, just as having homosexual thoughts or dreams does not necessarily mean that a person is gay or lesbian.

Gay men and lesbians have existed in every culture and society. Some societies accept the incidence of homosexuality as natural, while others label it abnormal.

Homosexuals exist in every stratum of society—among the rich and poor, the educated and uneducated. They work in every imaginable profession. They are doctors, lawyers, politicians, police officers, mechanics, hairdressers, construction workers, athletes, and artists. Think what the world would be like without the genius of Michelangelo, Andy Warhol, Keith Haring, Cecil Beaton, Tchaikovsky, Diaghilev, Walt Whitman, Oscar Wilde, E. M. Forster, Gertrude Stein, Truman Capote, and James Baldwin.

People who taunt or attack homosexuals often do so out of ignorance and fear. Prejudice against homosexuals (homophobia) may stem from feelings of insecurity about one's own sexuality.

Homophobia can make life difficult for gays and lesbians. Still, most homosexuals, like other people who are discriminated against, adjust and become productive members of society. Many find love and companionship with lifelong partners.

If you have decided that you are homosexual, one of the most difficult issues you will face is whether to "come out" (let people know). If parents and friends react with understanding, "coming out" can strengthen these important relationships. But there are some cautions about "coming out." First of all you must realize that few parents who discover that their child is gay or lesbian are delighted. They might say something like "Where did I go wrong?" or "It's just a phase; you'll grow out of it" or "You're sick; you need a psychiatrist." If you know what to expect, you can prepare yourself to be patient and to teach them some of the facts about homosexuality.

Before you "come out" to your friends and peers, be sure to think about the probable reactions of those closest to you. Consider whether they can be trusted with this most personal information. Your sexual identity is your own business, and you have the right to be as protective of yourself as you think is necessary. Some parents and friends may not understand and may overreact. Once you, your family, and your friends accept your orientation, which can sometimes take a long time, you will feel better about yourself. Staying "in the closet" means hiding parts of yourself from those you care about. Even when this is done for a good reason, it can create stress and negative feelings because of the deception that is often perceived to be taking place.

If you choose to "come out," select a time that *you* think is best and most appropriate for your family. Do not blurt out the revelation during an argument about something trivial (such as the use of the family car) or at an inappropriate time (such as a holiday meal, when all the relatives have gathered around your family's dining table).

Most parents who love their children come to accept them as homosexuals. If your parents reject you, try to help them accept the situation, but be aware that you may not be successful. Keep in mind that in the final analysis, it is your acceptance of yourself that really counts.

It is tragic that a significant number of gays and lesbians have attempted or have actually committed suicide because of guilt, fear, or societal pressure. Please read the following message that I received from a teenager who wanted you to know his story.

> You may be having suicidal feelings because you think you are gay. I know how you feel because I have had the same feelings. It is very frightening to think that some of your friends make jokes and comments that ridicule homosexuality.
>
> You may feel that you don't want to tell anyone about your feelings. I know that I thought my friends and family would never understand. But keeping your fears bottled up will only make you feel more depressed and alone. The support of trusted friends will help you. Talk with someone you like and trust—your rabbi, a teacher, a relative, a friend. Make the choice based on who you feel will be the most supportive and understanding. You may also wish to find a psychologist or

psychiatrist for professional counseling.

My closest friends and immediate family know now that I am gay and they have all assured me of their support. I only told them after I attempted to kill myself. I know now that I could have had their support all along and saved us all a great deal of anguish. So don't assume that others will "hate" you if you are gay. Give your friends a chance to be your friend.

If you notice suicidal feelings, ask yourself, do I really believe that I deserve to die for having homosexual feelings? The question is almost too ridiculous to answer. Of course you don't!

You may be gay and you may not be. Many people have homosexual experiences and then go on to lead heterosexual lives. You will not know who you are until you overcome the fear and anxiety and allow yourself the time and space to explore your sexual orientation.

You may think that if you are gay you will suddenly be transformed into the stereotype of gay men: effeminate, talking with a lisp, meeting other gays in the men's room. Don't be taken in by crude stereotypes. It is quite possible to lead a full, successful, and happy life as a homosexual. There are people with stable and loving sex lives among both heterosexuals and homosexuals, and there are people with promiscuous sex lives among both heterosexuals and homosexuals.

It will be helpful to you to read novels, see films, or read nonfiction on homosexuality. This will make the topic of homosexuality less threatening and mysterious to you.

Your process of finding your sexual orientation *will* be difficult and at times painful. Don't make it more difficult by keeping all your worries to yourself and thus taking the risk of falling into a serious, or even suicidal, depression.

If you are troubled about homosexuality, find a sympathetic counselor with whom you can talk. Stay away from those who claim they can "cure" homosexuality and from people who are homophobic. One way to find a person with whom you can talk is through your local gay and lesbian hot line. Almost every major city in the country has one. Look in the telephone book. In New York City the telephone number of the Hetrick Martin Institute at 401 West Street, New York, NY 10014-2587 is 212-633-8920. The institute was founded some years ago to help confused or troubled gay, lesbian, and bisexual teens.

Anyone who is concerned about homosexuality should read *A Disturbed Peace* by Brian R. McNaught (St. Martin's Press, 1992). Recommended books for parents whose child is homosexual (or who are worried about that possibility) include *Now That You Know: What Every Parent Should Know about Homosexuality* by B. Fairchild and N. Hayward (Harcourt Brace, 1979), *Are You Still My Mother?* by Gloria Guss Back (Warner Books, 1985), *Bridges of Respect* by Katherine Whitlock (American Friends Service Committee, 1989), and *Twice Blessed—On Being Lesbian or Gay and Jewish* edited by Christie Ballsa and Andy Rose (Beacon Press, 1991).

Parents can get in touch with a local chapter of PFLAG (Parents and Friends of Lesbians and Gays) or write to that organization. The address is Post Office Box 27605, Central Station, Washington, D.C. 20048-7605.

Think you're pregnant? To be certain, you might begin with a home test. If your test is positive, see a doctor. Being pregnant is bad news if you don't want to be. But it's not the worst thing in the world. Talk to your parents. Most parents will help. If you feel you absolutely can't confide in your parents, then go to a Planned Parenthood Center or a family planning counselor. If you are opposed to abortion, go to a Birthright Clinic. It is your choice to have an abortion or complete the pregnancy. A good counselor will help you to make your decision without influencing you either way.

The main thing is that you don't do anything to hurt yourself because of your pregnancy. Why punish yourself twice? If you've made an error in judgment, turn it into a lesson, not a tragedy. Learn more about birth control and risky sexual behavior, and then use the information to avoid making the same mistake again.

About 50 percent of females and 70 percent of males are likely to have sexual intercourse before they are eighteen.

Those who remain virgins are often maligned by their peers.

I believe that virgins also have rights and that they ought to be respected for the courage to stand by their convictions.

As a psychologist, I am frequently asked if it is normal to postpone sex until marriage. I reply yes but add, "If you are going to wait, I trust you won't expect simultaneous orgasms on your wedding night. The decision to put off sex until marriage is a moral value and as such has nothing to do with fulfillment or pleasure."

Because human sexual pleasure and response are primarily learned activities, a person's first sexual experiences should not be taken lightly. Obtaining responsible answers to the questions "When? "Why?" and "With whom?" is important.

If I were to cite some of the most important characteristics of a good marriage, the list would include:
- Love, sensitivity, caring, and respect
- A sense of humor
- Sexual intercourse
- Sharing household tasks*

---

*If my ideas interest you, read *Why Love Is Not Enough* (Bob Adams, Inc.). Add your own ideas to the list.

How can you tell if you are really in love?

Most people confuse sex with love. There are people who have exciting sex and don't even like each other and there are those who love each other but have uninspired sex lives. About the dumbest thing anyone can do is marry for sex or "chemistry," as it is often called. Even well-intentioned adults tell young people things like "If you have sex before your wedding, you'll have nothing to look forward to in marriage. There'll be no surprises." I say that if sex is the only thing to look forward to in a marriage, don't marry. It's not worth it.

Some say that love is blind. I say that it's blind for only twenty-four hours. Then you have to open up your eyes and see the person you are in love with. Love at first sight? Maybe, but better take another look. The plain fact is, if you feel that you are in love, you are. But there are two kinds of love—mature and immature. It's not difficult to tell the difference. Mature love is energizing. Immature love is exhausting. An immature relationship tends to leave you tired. You procrastinate a lot. You don't do your schoolwork or your job well. You avoid your domestic responsibilities. ("Me? Wash the dishes? I can't do that. I'm in love!") You have what is called a hostile-dependent relationship. You can't bear to be away from the person you think you are in love with. But when you are together, you fight and argue most of the time. Mood swings and accusations of jealousy, even violence, characterize the relationship. Some people even confuse love and hate because of the emotional "charge" that they feel. But if someone beats you up or forces sex upon you, that is not real love. It's neurosis, dependency, or fear but not love. In an immature relationship one person usually repeatedly asks, "Do you love me? Do you really love me?" I advise the other person to say, "No." It'll be your first real conversation.

Immature relationships are characterized by promises like "Don't worry, honey, when we get married, I'll stop fooling around with other women [men]." You might as well know now: A bad situation is *always* made worse by marriage.

Immature relationships reveal insensitivity and selfishness by one or both partners. In such a relationship one person is always trying to meet the needs of the other and neither is satisfied. Love feels like a burden. When Sally says that she has a headache, Don is angry and replies: "Of course you have to get a headache on *my* day off." In a mature relationship Sally's headache elicits the following response: "I'm sorry that you have a headache. I'll get you an aspirin. We can have sex tomorrow."

Mature relationships are full of energy. You have time to do almost everything you want to do. You don't shirk responsibilities. When you are together, you enjoy each other. You might argue sometimes but not that much. You want to please each other.

How can you tell if what you feel is infatuation or mature love? In the first month you can't. (In the summer it takes two months.) Infatuation and mature love appear and feel exactly the same. But when the relationship settles in, all or some of the above-mentioned signs will appear, and you will be able to tell if you are *really* in love.

Here are some good general rules: Sex is never a test or proof of love. You can't buy love with sex. So many females, even in these enlightened times, have sex because it might lead to love, but many more males have sex because that is all that they want. A large number of males find it easier to make out than to make conversation. I'm not anti-male. I know that what I've written about males is also true of some females. It's just that many males are programmed by warped societal messages to exploit females.

So until men and women stop playing games with each other, it is important for you to know the rules of the games and decide whether or not you want to play. You can always take a time-out for honest communication.

Of course, many relationships start out with elements of immaturity but become mature as a result of a lot of caring and effort (and others start out mature and become angry and hostile). The key point here is that a mature relationship is an evolving, not always easy or magical, process.

MATURE LOVE NURTURES.
IMMATURE LOVE CAUSES PAIN.

Don't!

If you *truly* love anyone—your parents, your friends—you won't kill yourself. No matter how shabbily you feel that you have been treated by someone you care about, would you really want to bring such horrible pain to those whom you honestly love? They don't deserve it! You don't deserve it! If you feel desperate as a result of a fight or a breakup with someone you care about, don't act immediately. The emotions you are feeling will subside in time, and your view of what has happened will probably change dramatically. Give yourself and those you love a break. Sentencing yourself to death is not a rational move. Get help and talk the whole thing out with someone you trust. Don't take your life while you are in the middle of an emotional crisis. Your view of what has happened to you will change in time. Give yourself the gift of time.

When Scott Difiglia, a teenager from Plano, Texas, committed suicide because his girlfriend Kathy rejected him, he wrote a letter telling why he couldn't live with himself any longer. He concluded:

> I am really sorry for letting everybody
> down. Mom and Dad, I really love you a lot
> and I am really sorry. Thanks for putting
> up with all my shit for so long.
>
> *All my love forever,*
> *Scott*

What Scott did had nothing to do with his love for Kathy or his parents, however sincere he felt about it.* Real love *always, always* means that a person cares more about the people he or she loves and their needs than about his or her own feelings. Scott's actions stemmed from selfishness and self-hatred.

We mourn for Scott, but we mourn for his family and Kathy even more.

---

*See the article about Scott in *Rolling Stone*, November 8, 1984. (While this article was published a long time ago, Scott Difiglia's story remains a very tragic example of the consequences of misguided thinking.)

4

For Young People
Who Have "Problem Parents";
For Parents Who Have
"Problem Children"

If you don't get along with your parents

It is possible that your parents don't understand you.
It is possible that you are more adequate than your
parents are.
It is possible that your parents don't care about you or
are abusive.

But in 90 percent of cases, parents do care, or at least
one parent does. They do love you. But sometimes they
don't know what's right for you or how to express it.
Sometimes they are so preoccupied with their own troubles that they lose sight of yours. All parents have periods
of time when they honestly don't understand their kids.

If a particular problem is not very serious, ask your parents to read the section titled "A message to parents: don't
turn off your kids" (page 89). But before that read "A
message to teenagers: don't turn off your parents" (page
84).

If you feel you can't talk with your parents or if you think they just don't understand you, it's still important for them to at least listen to you. You may need to do something dramatic to get them to pay attention to you. Cut out the messages below (or write your own) and leave them around where your parents can find them. Pick the time carefully. And then risk telling one or both your parents how you feel. Don't hold anything back. It's possible that it won't work. But at least you tried.

Don't give up. There may be other opportunities to reach out to your parents. But in the end you may have to manage without parental support. Sometimes you may have to count on a friend's parents for help. It's still possible to manage. Don't try to take revenge. Your parents may need your forgiveness. Remember what we've said before: The best revenge is living well.

If you don't have the parents you want now, when you become a father or mother, become the father or mother you would have liked to have had.

Dear Mom,
I'm in deep trouble.
I need to talk to you.
I want you to listen to me
 without criticizing me.
It's important.

Dear Dad,
I'm in deep trouble.
I need to talk to you.
I want you to listen to me
 without criticizing me.
It's important.

A message to teenagers:
don't turn off your parents

One of the most difficult concepts for many young people to accept is that their parents are good people.* Most parents mean well even if they seem old-fashioned and don't always make sense to their children. To you, parental restrictions may seem like hostility; to your parents, they represent concern for you.

Whether you like it or not, getting along with parents generally is an essential aspect of becoming a reasonably well-adjusted adult. It's true that in some cases young people are better adjusted than their parents. Although it is still possible for these young people to manage in life, it takes a lot of courage.

So if you've had some stormy times with your parents lately and especially if you feel they are not listening to you, here are a few surefire suggestions that almost all parents would appreciate.

- Make it a point to spend a couple of hours a week with your parents. Talk to them about anything or just watch TV with them, but be sure to talk to them during the commercials.
- Every once in a while ask a parent who works outside the home, "How are things going?" (If he or she answers, "Fine," say, "I mean, I'd like to hear more about your job/business.")
- Ask one or both parents for advice about something not too crucial so that you can easily follow their suggestions.

---

*Some parents, of course, are abusive. If your parents fall into this category, it's up to you to "rise above" them. The situation is not your fault so don't punish yourself twice.

- Experiment with telling the truth about aspects of your life that you have not been truthful about. If necessary, start by saying, "I worry that if I tell you the truth, you'll be very upset" or "When I tell the truth, the whole thing gets blown up out of proportion, so I am reluctant to be honest and open with you."
- Clean up your room at unexpected times.
- Take out the garbage or do the dishes without being asked.
- Compliment your parents on things that they do well.

Another way of improving your relationship with your parents is to embark on a one-month politeness campaign. Make it a point to be polite without sounding phony or sarcastic. This may require some practice in front of your mirror. Say things like "Good morning," "Thank you," "Excuse me," and when you feel unusually generous, "I have a free hour. Is there a chore that you would like me to do?" You mom or dad may ask if you are feeling well after that one! Or they might say, "What's gotten into you?" or "What took you so long to decide you're human?" Your response might be, "I haven't been very considerate lately. I'm trying to change to see if being considerate will make things more pleasant."

Let the experiment continue for at least a month, and then evaluate the results. If you have been working toward something you want, ask for it in this way: "I'd like to talk with you about something. Please hear me out, and then I would like to hear your thoughts on the subject." You may discover in the process that politeness makes life much easier for you, even if you don't get what you want. Although being polite is not always a sure method of getting closer to your parents, it can be a way of keeping your distance, which, in time, will give you the opportunity to discover your own way. You may then decide to close the gap or maintain a polite relationship, but that's up to you.

This approach is contrived, but it's still a good way to end a period of noncommunication and improve relations at home. All adults appreciate even a little effort. If you don't think this is so, try this method on an irksome teacher.

Ask your grandparents to tell you about their parents. I regret that I never knew anything about my great-grandparents, pictured above.

Did a divorce or separation— or living with a stepparent—mess you up?

Divorce or separation affects millions of children living at home and away at college. The situation for a large number of young people often improves as a consequence of divorce. Living with one loving parent is a relief after surviving years of living with two parents who are constantly fighting, arguing, perhaps abusing each other, and sometimes abusing the children as well. Many young people from broken families have found themselves in really bad circumstances for various reasons. These children of separated or divorced parents

- feel deprived
- face economic hardship
- have many added responsibilities
- miss the absent parent
- are caught in the middle and are sometimes forced to take sides
- feel angry or abandoned
- are so worried about the divorce or separation that their schoolwork and friendships are affected
- feel guilty in a way that isn't constructive

If any one of these or related issues have affected you, here are some things that you can do and ideas that you can think about.

First and foremost you must recognize that if your parents break up, *it's not your fault.* You are not responsible even if a parent in an angry, impulsive moment blames you.

Life may be tough right now. Life may seem unfair. You may feel depressed, but that's not a reason to punish yourself twice. It's unfortunate that you don't have the family life you want, but that's not a reason to fail in school, be rotten to the people you live with, or do things that are self-destructive (like taking drugs). You need to resolve and insure that you won't make a bad situation worse by hurting yourself. *Now* is particularly the time to protect yourself, to be nice to yourself. Try at least to be polite to a parent or stepparent you don't like. Your attitude might change if you acquire more understanding or make an effort to forgive.

In any case, however far off it may seem, you will soon be working or in college. You'll be able to make your own decisions, live your own life, marry, and have children of your own. The *only* way you can achieve all this is by preparing yourself now. Get the grades you want and earn the money you need.

You may have to postpone some pleasures. You will have to avoid inadequate "solutions," like alcohol. You will need to practice patience and learn to tolerate frustration. But that does not mean your life has to be grim. You can still have relationships. Try to develop at least one intimate friendship. You need someone in whom you can confide. Develop an interest in at least one thing you can be passionate about. Be helpful to at least one person more vulnerable than you are. Make a commitment to at least one cause.

By reaching out beyond your own (perhaps even really bad) situation, you could be a source of comfort to others and, strange as it may seem, an inspiration to yourself. You will feel energized.

A message to parents:
don't turn off your kids

No, you don't have to compromise your values.

No, you don't have to shift from being old-fashioned (which most parents are) to being what people call progressive, liberal, or "with it."

Yes, you may have to improve your communication skills.

First you must recognize that adolescence is not a disease or a terrible stage that all young people go through. Many young people actually enjoy their adolescence.

Teenagers need to be appreciated and accepted as family decision makers. They should be in on problems, even serious ones, such as unemployment, fatal illnesses, and impending divorce. Teenagers feel rejected if they are excluded from family conferences. They need to have parents who are available to listen to their problems and take them seriously.

Never, never make fun of or mock a teenager's love affair. Young people's feelings are as strong as those of mature adults but are generally of shorter duration. It doesn't matter one bit if you are sure that the relationship won't last.

Please don't say things like "You'll get over it" or "When you get older you'll laugh about this" or "It's just puppy love."

It's all right not to like your child's friends or choice of boyfriend or girlfriend. State your feelings, especially if a particular relationship seems to be having a bad effect on your child's attitude toward school or within the home environment (for example, if the child is using this relationship as an excuse to get out of responsibilities).

You can simply state that in your opinion good relationships are "contagious." They make people feel good about themselves and are energizing. People in good relationships do well in school and can afford to be responsive to their parents.

But no matter how you feel, you should always be polite to your teenager and to his or her friends.

THE MOST IMPORTANT RULE IS:
NEVER, NEVER BREAK OFF COMMUNICATION
WITH YOUR CHILDREN,
NO MATTER WHAT THEY DO.

This does not mean that you can't express how you feel about a particular situation. And try not to have a standard response to almost all crises.

I asked my college students to recall a single sentence that most characterized what they considered as inappropriate parental responses to a serious problem they had. A surprisingly large percentage of students, even those who claimed they got along reasonably well with their parents, recalled sentences like:

From mothers
- Life is tough all over.
- Count your blessings.
- Where did I go wrong?
- Go ask your father.
- Shut off the noise box.

From fathers
- Life isn't fair.
- Moderation, moderation.
- For crying out loud.
- Go ask your mother.
- Life is too short to be miserable.

If you want to have a serious talk with your child, please don't start with the following (which are guaranteed to turn off young people):
- When I was your age . . .

- It's about time you got good grades (*or* straightened up your room).
- That's not your idea, is it?
- Wipe that smile off your face.
- After all we've done for you!
- What will the neighbors say?
- Are you telling me the truth?
- Act your age.
- As long as I don't know about it.
- Get off your high horse.

And please, don't ever tell a teenager not to worry. When was the last time someone told you not to worry and you stopped?

You may have teenagers who do a lot of things you disapprove of: They don't clean their room, they don't take their homework seriously, and they watch too much television.

Try to make a point of dealing with one thing at a time. Concentrate on only one or two issues and temporarily ignore everything else. This is usually a successful response only if you try at the same time to improve the quality of your relationship with your teenager by becoming involved in experiences together.

Telling teenagers all the "don'ts"—don't smoke, drink, get high, have sex, or stay out late—doesn't accomplish much unless we can help them discover positive ways to behave that will make them feel good about themselves.

It is not surprising that parents often label certain behavior rebellious, spiteful, ungrateful, or spoiled. Parental concerns are magnified when the misbehavior occurs on a daily basis.

Many parents tend to talk too much and complain about the whole spectrum of problems instead of concentrating on a specific issue or issues.

Suppose the main problem is that your teenager chronically stays out late and does not come home at the prescribed time. On one particular occasion the teen had promised to be home on time but comes home an hour late without having telephoned. The parent is waiting up, furious that a promise has been broken and worried about the child's safety. As the teenager approaches the front door, he or she reviews his or her made-up explanation for being late (a broken-down car and a traffic jam are old favorites).

After having had a good time with friends, the teenager arrives home tense and anxious, anticipating the confrontation. The parents' own anxiety has built to the boiling point as a result of hours of fretting and the fact that the teen has been late practically every Saturday night for the past two months. During the fight that begins as soon as the door is opened, no constructive communication takes place. What the parents' anger is saying to the teenager is, "We don't trust you. You are a louse for making us so upset." Often the punishment administered is too severe for the offense. If grounding works, fine, but first evaluate the duration and effectiveness of the punishment and the possible dissension it can create.

The next time your teen is late, say, "I'm very disappointed that you didn't keep your promise" and then leave the room. This is sure to generate guilt. Please realize that a prolonged shouting match will dissipate any guilt your teenager might feel.

There is nothing wrong with generating guilt in a teenager who has misbehaved. It's nonsensical to argue that all guilt is undesirable. Irrational guilt that overwhelms a person is not helpful, but rational guilt, which organizes a person and helps him or her avoid repetition of undesirable behavior, can be a constructive force—at least until the hoped-for "good judgment" kicks in.

At this point I would like to state my opposition to physical punishment under any circumstances. It tends to create even more anger and alienation and to intensify conflict. Few things turn kids off more than a slap across the face.

Sometimes parents forget that adolescents need models more than they need critics. They want their parents to respect their integrity and privacy and to include them in family matters. Above all, perhaps, they want love that they can return and information that can lead to self-acquired wisdom.

If your child shuts you out, knock gently on his or her door and say softly, "Honey, I love you. I really need to talk!" or "Do you need a hug? I sure do!" or "I want to understand what just happened between us. Please help me."

Persist even if you are told to go away.

Don't wait for a crisis to tell your child that you love him or her. All of us, *even* the most independent teenagers, need hugs and kisses, or at least a friendly pat.

Be sure your teen knows that you are always going to help and support him or her. No matter how awful the crisis, you will not turn your back on your child. Rejection is not a part of a parent's role. You may not accept some behaviors, but the person is not the behavior. If your child thinks that you are always misunderstanding him or her or that your responses are somehow "off the wall," ask your child to tell you and then try to change your approach. If nothing else, this change might improve communication between you. The more respect you show your teen, the more respect you will get.

If you tell kids that they will never amount to anything or that they are stupid, they might believe you.

Don't give your children the impression that they have only one option. Try not to say things like "If you don't go to college [don't pass math], you're doomed." It is better if you say, "It's my [our] hope that you will go to college [pass math with flying colors, or whatever]. If that is not going to happen, we need to discuss alternatives, and I think I can offer some help."

Please don't compare your children. Above all, allow your children to express what they feel, whether it is unhappiness, disappointment, sadness, or joy. The feelings belong to them, and you don't have to share them, just accept them. Trying to understand a teenager can be hard work, especially when you remember how easy life was with this same person just a few years ago, but the rewards are worth it. I believe that the more sensitive we are to young people today, the more they are going to try to understand and be understanding in the future.

The main responsibilities of parents to their children are to

- love them
- talk openly with them
- nurture them
- help them turn their mistakes into lessons
- promote their self-esteem

Parents who take these responsibilities seriously have a good chance of raising independent adults who will feel affection and love for their parents.

Please note: The overwhelming majority of parents mean well and love their children, but nobody can be a perfect parent. When the uniqueness of each child, birth order, parental age (young or old), changing family circumstances, and a host of other variables are all taken into account, it is a tribute to human nature that any of us turns out to be "normal." Jerome Kagan, a noted psychologist, stresses in his book *The Nature of the Child* (Basic

Books) that we have greatly overemphasized the role of parents as *the* determining factor in how children develop. Parents are important, of course, but so is the fact that children are born differentially fearful, irritable, and alert. Their peers and the media also influence them.

The majority of mothers tend to blame themselves for whatever happens. They also tend to receive most of the praise if things work out well, even though today's fathers are much more involved in child-rearing. I recommend that mothers read Lynn Caine's book *What Did I Do Wrong? Mothers, Children, Guilt* (Arbor House).

For parents who have "out of control" children, I recommend contacting Toughlove. To find a group in your area, call 215-348-7090, or write to Toughlove, Box 1069, Doylestown, PA 18901.

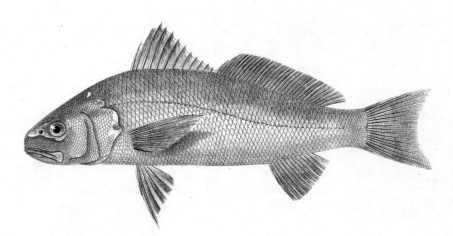

5

God Concerns

Are you disappointed in God?

First you need to know that God can't do everything. We can't ask God to change the rules of nature for our benefit. God does, however, help those who stop hurting themselves.

Rabbi Harold S. Kushner expounded on these ideas in his wonderfully warm, deeply religious book titled *When Bad Things Happen to Good People* (Avon Books, 1983), which he wrote after experiencing a personal tragedy.

Rabbi Kushner says that God might not prevent calamity but God does give us the strength and the perseverance to overcome it.

> Prayer cannot bring water to parched fields, nor mend a broken bridge, nor rebuild a ruined city; but prayer can water an arid soul, mend a broken heart, and rebuild a weakened will.
>
> —*Gates of Prayer*

Rejecting religion is understandable if you expect faith to alter natural events but discover that it does not, or if you believe that God will allow only good things to happen to you but you are instead experiencing many problems. Only you can give yourself a good life.

It is, however, appropriate to agonize over why your religion hasn't helped you feel better about yourself. Discuss the issue with your rabbi, priest, or minister. You might get some surprising answers.

Having a meaningful religious identity can help you feel better about yourself and others.

Here is what I think.

There is a way for everyone

People who want to mock God
    say there is only
    one road to heaven.
God knows
    a one-way sign is a
    dead end,
    leading to nowhere.
God knows
    there are infinite ways to find
    your own way.

John Donne, a Roman Catholic priest, theologian, and philosopher, suggests that we give up the search for certainty and go on a voyage of discovery and understanding. He feels that the question to ask is not "Is there a God?" but rather "What is God?"

Do you feel in need of prayer?

When heavy burdens oppress us and our spirits grow faint and the gloom of failure settles upon us, help us to see through the darkness to the light beyond.

To You, O God, we turn for light; turn to us and help us.

When we come to doubt the value of life because suffering blinds us to life's goodness, give us the understanding to bear pain without despair.

To You, O God, we turn for understanding; turn to us and help us.

When we are tempted to suppress the voice of conscience, to call evil good and good evil, turn our hearts to the rights of others and make us more responsive to their needs.

To You, O God, we turn for guidance; turn to us and help us.

And when we become immersed in material cares and worldly pleasures, forgetting You, may we find that all things bear witness to You, O God, and let them lead us back into Your presence.

To You, O God, we turn for meaning; turn to us and help us.

—*Gates of Prayer*

Looking inward, I see that all too often I fail to use time and talent to improve myself and to serve others. And yet there is in me much goodness and a yearning to use my gifts for the well-being of those around me. This Sabbath [*or* day] calls me to renew my vision, to fulfill the best that is within me. For this I look to God for help.

Give meaning to my life and substance to my hopes; help me understand those around me and fill me with the desire to serve them. Let me not forget that I depend on others as they depend on me; quicken my heart and hand to lift them up; make faithful my words of prayer, that they may fulfill themselves in deeds.

—Gates of Prayer

6

What Is the
Purpose of Life?

Does life have a purpose?

Martin Buber, reflecting on the philosophy of the Baal Shem Tov, the great chasidic master, suggested that every person born into this world represents something new, something that never existed before.

All of us have the task of actualizing our unprecedented and never-recurring potentiality and not the repetition of something that another has already achieved. Everyone is unique because had there ever been anyone like you, there would be no need for you in the world.*

I was blown away when I read the Baal Shem Tov's powerful statement of purpose for each of us. It immediately reinforced my belief that not only was I unique and special, I also had a mission. And while I could never be fully certain what that mission's exact nature was, I *knew* that I was on the right track when the following words came to me.

---

*Read *The Way of Man According to the Teaching of Hasidism* by Martin Buber (The Citadel Press, 1950).

Everybody
is
unique.
Compare not
yourself
to anybody else,
lest
you spoil
God's curriculum.

My becoming a writer didn't depend on anyone else's agreeing that I should be one. If you are on the right path, one person is a majority. (Marilyn Ferguson's *The Aquarian Conspiracy* set me thinking along these lines.)

Viktor E. Frankl has explored in depth the meaning of life in his remarkable book *Man's Search for Meaning* (Touchstone, revised 1984). Frankl, a psychiatrist and Holocaust survivor, argues that the meaning of life is always changing. One can discover its varying meanings in three different ways.

- By creating a work or doing a deed, that is, by some achievement or accomplishment
- By experiencing goodness, truth in nature, culture, and most of all by loving another human being
- By transforming a personal tragedy into a triumph, turning one's predicament into a human achievement

Frankl concludes that at its best, human potential will always allow for

- turning suffering into an achievement
- deriving from guilt the ability to change oneself for the better
- finding an incentive for action. There is never a good reason to be *stuck* in any kind of suffering. The potential for change is always present

Here is Frankl's advice to all of us.

> Don't aim at success. The more you aim at it and make it a target, the more you are going to miss it. For success, like happiness, cannot be pursued. It must ensue, and it only does so as the unintended side effect of one's personal dedication to a cause greater than oneself or as the by-product of one's surrender to a person other than oneself.

Frankl sees "surrender" as the giving of ourselves to a loving relationship.

IT'S NOT GIVING UP, IT'S GIVING TO!
IN THE GIVING, YOU SHALL RECEIVE!

If someone asks you what is happening in your life, could you give a response that approximates one of the following answers?
- I'm in love.
- I'm an artist.
- I'm working for world peace.
- I'm into my schoolwork.
- I'm a big brother/sister to a little kid I care about.
- I've joined the Audubon Society.
- I work as a volunteer at the Children's Hospital.
- I'm excited about my home computer.

Without a sense of purpose, life doesn't seem very exciting or meaningful. That's why so many people end up filling the emptiness of their lives with despair, addiction to TV, sex, violence, drugs and alcohol, and passivity.

Here is the voice of a Holocaust survivor, Rabbi Arthur Schneier.

> I can say that if anything, I have been strengthened as a result of the Holocaust. Instead of just taking my energy and being bitter and resentful, I was able to harness this energy for positive bridge building with people of other faiths, with people of other ideological persuasions. That is the price I must pay for my survival.

Rage is destructive and renders survival meaningless. Forgiveness frees you to be your own person. It is energizing. It offers you another opportunity to be optimistic. You become a hero. Give it a try.

Start by forgiving your parents, a friend, or someone you love who has rejected or betrayed you. Often these people mean well, even if they hurt you. Don't they say, "I'm doing this for your own good"? But sometimes they know not what they are doing.

Hate is exhausting.

Forgiveness makes love possible again.

Just because you feel unloved now doesn't mean that you are unlovable.

If you can't forgive someone who hurt you or if you can't accept the idea of forgiveness

I do not believe that we must forgive everyone for every act. You may not want to forgive the rapist, the mugger, the people responsible for the Holocaust, but you should. For your own mental health if nothing else, forgive the people who have hurt you but did so without malicious or conscious intent, as well as those who realize their mistakes and ask your forgiveness.

As for those you cannot forgive—the rapist, the mugger, the murderer—why give them the ultimate victory by punishing yourself for years? Sure you'll be hurt and upset and might need help to recover. But recover fully you must. You must shout out, "I'm alive! I'll protect myself. Enough of suffering. I'll help others. I'm determined that this terrible event will not destroy my life. I will live well!"

A young friend of mine who made three suicide attempts before he was twenty-one objected to my emphasis on forgiveness. He is now thirty-five, very much alive, vibrant, creative, and thrilled that he didn't kill himself. He wrote:

> As I explored my spiritual being, I have succeeded in overcoming self-hatred by working with unconditional love, unconditional acceptance, and compassion. These concepts keep me spiritually equal to others and do not presume—which forgiveness does—that I'm better than anyone else.

He views compassion, not forgiveness, as the key. I'm not sure. But it's something to think about.

It's never too late

- To try again
- To grow again
- To share again
- To risk again
- To feel again
- To change again
- To love again
- To be enthusiastic again
- To read *Winnie the Pooh* for the first time

When someone you love has died

There are no rules. There are no stages you must go through. My friend Marian Leavitt says, "Every death has a life of its own."

I have been comforted by the following meditation. Perhaps you will be, too.

> It is hard to sing of oneness when our world is not complete, when those who once brought wholeness to our life have gone, and naught but memory can fill the emptiness their passing leaves behind.
>
> But memory can tell us only what we were in company with those we loved; it cannot help us find what each of us, alone, must now become. Yet no one is really alone; those who live no more echo still within our thoughts and words, and what they did is part of what we have become.
>
> We do best homage to our dead when we live our lives most fully, even in the shadow of our loss. For each of our lives is worth the life of the whole world; in each one is the breath of the Ultimate One. In affirming the One, we affirm the worth of each one whose life, now ended, brought us closer to the Source of life, in whose unity no one is alone and every life finds purpose.
>
> —from *New Union Prayerbook*

It is renewed
- when we talk about our feelings
- when we confide in someone
- when we realize that we can influence our own lives
- when we develop relationships
- when we realize that all moods are temporary
- when we do mitzvot* and practice forgiveness

How can you tell when hope is being renewed? You'll feel energized and optimistic. You'll realize that the people who care about you are not complete without you!

---

*"good deeds"

7

More Fragments
of an Autobiography

Sometimes it takes
        the death of someone close,
an awareness,
        "There go I
        by the grace of God"
(I could have been gassed in the Holocaust),
a recovery from a terrible illness or accident,
        surviving a catastrophe
        or a "simple" mugging

to discover how marvelous it is
        just to be alive
        with all our imperfections.

Some people are lucky.
        They know this without
        being reminded by tragedies.

I've been reading *The Road Less Traveled* by M. Scott
Peck (Simon & Schuster, 1978). Peck sees life as a series of
problems that require resolution. He says that the difference between mature and immature people depends on
successful and unsuccessful resolution of problems. He

puts a heavy emphasis on discipline, and he helps us appreciate that the process of confronting and solving problems—a lifelong process—is painful. For him the whole process of meeting and solving problems is what makes life meaningful. Problems call forth our courage and wisdom. Carl Jung suggested, "Neurosis is always a substitute for legitimate suffering."

My friend Gloria Blum says, "There are no mistakes, only lessons."

How does one find peace in a dreadful world? I struggle with conflicting thoughts. They are not harmonious, and they don't all make sense. But we go on with our daily lives, of course, occupied with unimportant things. We don't spend time thinking about the things that are worth thinking about. The Talmud says, "Just as the hand held before the eye can hide the tallest mountain, so the routine of everyday life can keep us from seeing the vast radiance and the secret wonders that fill the world." The author William James wrote, "Wisdom is learning what to overlook." It's a matter of struggling with priorities, finding out what's important, what your particular mission in life is.

We each have a responsibility to find out what meaning life has for us, knowing full well that this is a lifelong process. How can we put to use our uniqueness to develop ourselves and in the process be useful and helpful to others? Many people today are depressed mainly because they feel useless.

Surely we have to do our daily tasks, even though many of them are boring. The most meaningful and joyous experiences in life are of brief duration. But what are we to do in the meantime?

I think we have to do more mitzvot, "good deeds."

I think we need to reduce our fear of vulnerability by exposing ourselves to uncertainty—by taking risks.

As Gertrude Stein suggested on her deathbed, we don't need the answer, we need the question. We need to find the way to the question. If the way is not clear, we need to make our own.

A stunning book titled *Number Our Days* by Barbara Meyerhoff (Simon & Schuster, 1980) includes the following passage:

> "A man of great wisdom, a doctor told me I had a fatal disease. 'You cannot remedy it,' he said. 'There is nothing I can do for you except to give you this advice: Do your work as well as you can. Love those around you. Know what you are doing. Go home and live fully. The fatal disease is life.'"
>
> "This is very interesting," Shmuel said. "The Jews do not have much of an idea about afterlife. Everything is how you live here. You should be good to others. You should pay attention to your history. You should always be wide-awake so you can be responsible for what you do. God wants more of the Jews than to survive. The Jews must choose to be alive. So for once, I would have to say you had a very Jewish dream."

I live my life almost fully and with energy, but I have some regrets, personal distresses, and genuine disappointments. Suffering is personal and cannot easily be shared.

My survival depends upon
    a sense of humor
    a sense of purpose
    a sense of mission
    a sense of meaning
    a sense of beauty
    a sense of nonsense
    a common sense

a passion for *bittersweet*
        plays
        ballet
        movies
        music
        art
        novels
        chocolate and
        intimacy

June 12 is my birthday. Send bittersweet greetings.

What's a mensch?

Without aspiring to
be a
mensch,
being alive is a
burden.

We all start out human.
No way can we be more so
or less so.

We are at all times
struggling with the good and the bad
parts of ourselves.

Our free will represents the heart
of becoming a
mensch.

A mensch is someone who
aspires to be
a good person
and is,
most of the time.
A good person is
someone who accepts the biblical injunction to
Love Thy Neighbor As Thyself.

This is not easy, especially for those
who don't love themselves.
The best way to change
is by being nice to others;
then you may at least
feel good about yourself.

If you bless others,
you can then bless yourself.
If you can afford to see good in others,
you'll come to see good in yourself.

But there is still a catch.
Not everyone is in harmony
with your timing.
Not everyone is receptive
to your kindness.

A really important obligation
of a mensch is to do
mitzvot, "good deeds."
A person does mitzvot without expecting
something in return.
But mitzvot alway bring you rewards.

A mensch is a good person
who has faith in humanity
and expresses it with selfless love.

My mother (of blessed memory)
used to say to us in Yiddish,
Zug a gut vort. Est cost nit mare.
"Say a good word. It doesn't cost more."
She was a mensch.
My life is a struggle to become one.
The hardest part of becoming a mensch
is forgiveness.

New journeys, experiences, and people call forth a *new you*. Why eighteen? In Hebrew the word *chai* means "life," and its numerical value is eighteen. *Chai* is my favorite number.

1. *The existential question* is how you come to terms with life, not death.
2. You cannot find yourself through
   - drugs
   - dieting
   - complaining
   - getting laid
   - watching TV
   - movies
   - eating
   - jogging
   - making a fast buck
   - violence
     or in
   - bars
   - cults
   - parties

   Only through ongoing relationships with people can you find yourself.
3. Ridicule is making fun of other people's pain.
4. People who feel good about themselves (most of the time) do not allow themselves to be exploited, nor do they want to exploit others.
5. Not everything in life can be understood or resolved. All of us have some areas of vulnerability. Sometimes the best we can do isn't good enough. Some of us live in places where the winters are cold and long. That's why it's good to be optimistic.

6. Really marvelous experiences occur infrequently, do not last long, and are rarely scheduled.
7. "It is characteristic of wisdom not to do desperate things." (Henry David Thoreau)
8. Food can make you feel full, but fulfillment comes only with love.
9. If you have a tendency to put yourself down, struggle against it. It's boring to be with people who are down on themselves.
10. Each individual is a unique being beyond the reach of diagnostic categories, an artist overflowing with the will and freedom to shape his or her own fate. (Otto Rank)
11. It's easy to be a hero in someone else's situation.
12. Intimacy is joyous and sad. It is sharing and open-ended, and it takes your mind off yourself momentarily.
13. In order to perfect oneself, one must renew oneself day by day. (a chasidic saying)
14. Love is where it's at and that's a fact. (a refrain from a not-yet-composed popular song)
15. "All the way to Heaven is Heaven." (Ste. Catherine)
16. "Honesty is not necessarily self-disclosure. It is saying *only* what you mean." (Sylvia Hacker)
17. Suffering may not enhance your life but recovery will.
18. Vibrations are real.

Thoughts and things to do
for the next eighteen days

Day one: Letting go of the ghosts of the past will permit you to have the life you're ready for today.

Day two: Let go of any thoughts that don't enhance your life.

Day three: Give someone the benefit of the doubt.

Day four: You don't have to prove yourself to anyone today.

Day five: Say no when you mean no. This frees you to mean yes when you say yes.

Day six: Offer a friend some of your energy.

Day seven: If you've wronged someone, ask that person to forgive you.

Day eight: Today say only what you mean.

Day nine: There is nothing you need to do first in order to be enlightened.

Day ten: Share a dream with someone.

Day eleven: Grow by coming to the end of something and by beginning something else.

Day twelve: Set yourself a simple task and complete it today.

Day thirteen: Express your appreciation to someone.

Day fourteen: Realize that maturity is the capacity to endure uncertainty.

Day fifteen: Teach someone something new.

Day sixteen: Turn one of your mistakes into a lesson.

Day seventeen: Expect a miracle but don't count on one.

Day eighteen: Seek peace in your own place. You cannot find peace anywhere except within yourself.

If you still don't feel better about yourself

Everybody has problems, but people who feel inferior seem to have more than their share.

Everybody is unique and has a particular mission in life. One of our sages is reported to have said on his deathbed, "God will not ask me why I was not like Moses. He will ask me why I wasn't myself."

Are you making the following seven cardinal mistakes?

1. Comparing yourself unfavorably with others. There will always be people who appear to be handsomer, richer, luckier, and better educated. We are all created equal in the eyes of God. We are all created different to serve God in a special way.
2. Feeling that you won't amount to much unless
   • someone falls for you
   • someone marries you
   • someone needs you
   • you earn a lot of money
   • your parents are satisfied with your achievements

You have to be *someone* to become attractive to someone else. You have to accept yourself before you can please someone you care about. If you don't amount to anything before someone wants you, you won't amount to much afterward.

3. Thinking you must please everyone. You must first please yourself and thereafter only those people you care about. People who try to please everyone end up pleasing no one.
4. Setting unreasonable goals for yourself. Lower your standards to improve your performance. You can al-

ways advance beyond today if you want to.

5. Looking for *the* meaning of life. Life is not a meaning. It is an opportunity. You can only find *the* meaning of life at the end of it. Life is made up of meaningful experiences that are mainly of short duration but repeatable.

6. Feeling bored. If you are bored, you are boring to be with. It is especially unattractive to bemoan how much you don't like yourself or how little you have to do. If you have nothing to do, don't do it here.

7. Deciding that your fate is determined by forces outside yourself. Maybe it is, but you can usually control your *attitude* about the difficult or good circumstances of your life. More often than not it is attitude that makes the difference.

People who feel good about themselves
- are enthusiastic
- have a sense of humor
- have interests
- enjoy being helpful
- are unselfish
- don't exploit others
- do not allow themselves to be exploited
- don't make fun of others
- have a sense of their own special mission
- can begin again
- turn their mistakes into lessons
- are optimistic
- are willing to take risks
- know how to listen
- make others feel good about themselves

How can you feel good about yourself? You can start by creating a miracle for yourself. Recognize that you are unique. Stop comparing yourself with other people. Believe that you can stand on your own merits.

When or if you have children, raise them to like themselves. That's the most important thing. Don't criticize them for things that they can't change. Don't force them to excel in areas in which they have no interest or talent. Praise their uniqueness in small ways every day. Children who like themselves develop into adults who like themselves.

Be grateful for luck. Pay the thunder no mind—listen to the birds.
And don't hate nobody.

—Eubie Blake

When the mind is ready, a teacher appears.

—A Zen expression

Wisdom is learning what to overlook.

—William James

Nothing in life just happens. It isn't enough to believe in something. You have to have stamina to meet obstacles and overcome them, to struggle . . .

—Golda Meir

A person will be called to account on judgment day for every permissible thing that he or she might have enjoyed but did not.

—Jerusalem Talmud

Friendship is born at the moment when one person says to another, "What! You, too? I thought I was the only one."

—C. S. Lewis

Repeat over and over again,
"I shall either find a way or make one."
Or, in Latin, if you prefer,
Aut inveniam viam aut faciam.

And then say,
"I will be gentle with myself,
I will love myself,
I am part of the universe."

—Joseph and Nathan

One person of integrity can make a difference.

—Elie Wiesel

The best thing you can do for yourself is to forgive yourself. There'll be plenty of sunuvabitches to beat on you and say ugly things. Guilt is a loser's game. You can't get back yesterday, or even this afternoon.

—Harry Crews,
author of *A Childhood:*
The Biography of a Place

Crews adds, "The only way to deal with the real world was to challenge it with one of your own making."

Here are some thoughts that I had as I was putting the final touches on this book.

- Everybody makes mistakes. Turn mistakes into lessons.
- You are not alone. It only seems that way sometimes. Many people have the same feelings that you have.
- It's not your feelings that get you in trouble. It's your method of escape.

- We need to learn to accept our limitations and our emotional frailties.
- No one has the right to put you down for being different. Why be ordinary if you can be different?
- Accept criticism only from people you respect.
- Why put yourself down when there are plenty of mean people who will do it for you? Why give them any thought at all?
- Why travel heavy if you can travel light?
- Life is uncertain. Eat dessert first.

The Rules

1. Never judge a day by the weather.
2. The best things in life aren't things.
3. Tell the truth—There is less to remember.
4. Speak softly and wear a loud shirt.
5. Loosen up—The unaimed arrow never misses.
6. He who dies with the most toys—Still dies.
7. Age is relative—When you're over the hill— You pick up speed.
8. There are two ways to get rich—You can make more or you can require less.
9. What you look like doesn't matter—Beauty is internal.
10. No Rain—No Rainbows.

—Anonymous

Where to Go for Help

If you are in trouble now, and you can't reach any-one you trust, dial your local telephone operator. (Just dial 0.) Ask for Crisis or Help or Suicide Hot Lines in your area. If it's urgent, say, "I am in crisis, now!" If you get a busy signal, try again. Just imagine for a moment that someone else is in more trouble than you are (even if you don't think that this is possible). If the line remains busy, find an alternative crisis number by looking in the front pages of your telephone book for Emergency Crisis Hot Lines or Community Resources.